The new CEO
Dynamics of the changing Corporate

The new CEO

Dynamics of the changing Corporate

V. M. Budhiraja

India Research Press
New Delhi

India Research Press
B-4/22, Safdarjung Enclave,
New Delhi – 110 029.
Ph.: 24694610; Fax : 24618637
bahrisons@vsnl.com
contact@indiaresearchpress.com
www.indiaresearchpress.com

2004

ISBN : 81-87943-42-4

Cataloguing in Publication Data
V. M. Budhiraja
The new CEO Dynamics of the changing Corporate
V. M. Budhiraja

Includes references and index.

ISBN : 81-87943-42-4

1. Management 2. Corporate 3. CEO
4 . Title 5. Author

Printed at Focus Impressions, New Delhi – 110 003.

INTRODUCTION

The business corporations are witnessing a constant process of evolution and revolution. Sometimes the change is slow and at other times it could be radical and drastic. The various factors which impinge on the shape, size, strategy, structure and operating practices of a corporation have direct and dynamic links with the social, economic and political conditions of a country. The social aspects determine the operating culture of a business enterprise and help to evolve the process of management in the shape of structure, systems and inter relationship amongst the various segments of the corporation as also installing mechanisms for supervision, control, empowerment and other similar processes.

The economic situation decides the tenor of business-related policies regarding the area of focus of corporate activity, the type of products and the volume to be manufactured and distributed in the country, the quantum and destination of export and the nature of technology to be adopted for the various production processes, keeping in view the trade off between cost of capital and labour. It also directs to consider the demographic situation in the country, the type and level of employment to be provided, availability of trained and skilled man power in the category of workers, supervisory cadres, middle level executives and the top executives as also the macro and micro level man power policies of the government with regard to the employment of female and child labour in the various enterprises.

The business-related economic policies usually have orientation to the specific requirements of the country but also have some orientation to the economic conditions and business related guidelines established and commitments made at the international fora. Thus the changing economic scenario affects the corporate world in various ways.

The political climate of the country and the type of government enables the corporates to evolve suitable policies, processes and procedures in the context of rules and regulations directing the governance of business enterprises in the country. The political system helps as well as hinders the pace of growth of business and its focus of activity. Especially in a democratic set up, the political system has a deep impact on the modus operandi of business. The influence of the politicians, the government and the bureaucracy could be unimaginable. This is so particularly in the case of PSUs in India. The private enterprises too have witnessed the impact of the political forces from the days of Licence Raj to the present day environment of liberalization, modernization and globalization. The reform process initiated in the earlier decades too has impacted the corporate scenario considerably.

As the process of change has occurred in the socio-economic-cum-political spheres on a big scale in different parts of the world, an element of dynamism has been invested in the corporate affairs of the world.

At macro-level, the various changes which have been noticed in the corporate spheres relate to the process of structuring and restructuring, concept of value addition in the realms of production, manufacturing and services, benchmarking, corporate ethics and philosophy as well as the various aspects of corporate governance. These concepts and processes have assumed great importance for the efficient working and management of business enterprises.

At the level of individual business enterprises, the element of competition has assumed added importance. The various developments like corporate wars and celebrity endorsement have made themselves manifest in a big way.

On the HRD front, the various development like change in the job tenure, job-hopping, corporate hierarchy, structuring and restructuring, mergers and acquisitions, change in the corporate change order (in the context of slow and sudden change) are the aspects, which have gained importance in the last few decades. Also, the subject of succession for the executives, the CEOs and the entrepreneurs has assumed great significance in the scale of a corporation's concern.

Macro-level corporate mergers, acquisitions and take-overs within the country and abroad have become a normal feature of corporate life. Virtually, mega-mergers at the national and international level have become a routine affair. Whether the intention behind these mergers is to expand business or beat the competition, the story remains the same in different parts of the world. These mergers have created a great impact on the morale, motivation and job security of the employees as also other HR-related issues.

Bearing in mind the above perspective, the first part of the book comprising 18 chapters deals specifically with the subject of corporate dynamics and dilemma. The broad grouping in three categories, i.e. macro aspect, governance aspect and HRD aspect has been done to ensure an intergrated and focused approach on these issues.

Part II of the book which is entitled "CEOs' Universe" deals with different aspects like remunerations of a CEO, the role of a CEO, cultural orientation of a CEO and its impact on the decision-making process, skills and techniques relevant for the success of CEOs. The latest developments in the corporate life which have affected the psyche of the CEOs to a great extent have been incorporated in this part of the book. All told, there are 15 chapters on these topics including the subject of executive burnout which was mostly observed earlier at the level of middle or senior executives, who had failed to make the grade and achieve their career goals or other objects or purpose in life (at times also considered an extension of mid-life crisis) through the medium of a job in a business enterprise has now also affected the CEOs. This could be due to the impact of change in business paradigms caused by competition from the rivals and MNCs and the loss of image and face in the community and other stakeholders owing to recent corporate developments like scams and scandals. Hence this topic has also been included in the book. Part III contains case histories regarding succession, decision-making and ethics.

As some of the topics relating to developments in the earlier decades have been juxtaposed with the current situation, the book is likely to be highly relevant for the corporates taking responsibility for governance, supervision and execution. It will also be useful for the management faculty, academics and students of management. Politicians, bureaucrats and others associated with the control and regulation of business enterprises as also protecting the interests of various stakeholders could possibly draw useful cues from the state of affairs and set in motion the process of suitable ameliorative measures in this regard.

FOREWORD

The corporate world is witness to cataclysmic changes, powered in the main by the forces of economic liberalisation, modernisation and globalisation. Since the early 1980s, the grammar of business has expressed itself in terms like corporate restructuring, acquisitions, mergers and demergers, expressions that have country wide, and in many cases global, ramifications.

It is the competitive element that hyphenates all these exaperiences and the competition in turn spawned the language of value added services, competitive benchmarking, cutting - edge strategies and good corporate citizenship. Competition also translated into ceaseless price wars across industries, apart from giving a momentum to innovation, new technology, and modern production and marketing methods. For instance, Celebrity endorsements, part of today's brand positioning strategies, underscore the changing trends on the corporate landscape.

All these changes have left an indelible impring onthe human resource management plans of corporate entities. V M Budhiraja has captured these experiences in a highly interesting manner. The book is testimony to the author's rich experience in handling these inissues at various professional levels. He has dealt with various contemporary issues relating to the functioning of CEOs. It may be said that recent instances of moral turpitude of some of the leading MNC CEOs have tarnished the image of CEOs in general and put a question mark on the philosophy and practices of corporate governance. This book provides fresh insight into these issues.

Budhiraja's treatment of the subject is a reflection of of his own long stint with the government, MNCs, and public and privfate sector organisation, spanning 45 years. Needless to say, the text is a good blend of professional insight and journalistic flair.

Rajiv Raghunath
Resident Editor
The Financial World

Contents

PART-II : CEOs' UNIVERSE

PART-III : CASE HISTORIES

Part I

Corporate Dynamics

CHAPTER - 1

Corporate Restructuring

Restructuring — a corporate mantra of the business world — has assumed the dimension of almost a wave. PSUs, private limited companies as also family enterprises are seeking recourse to this expedient on the assumption that it will catapult their enterprise onto the path of Nirvana. While some are fiddling with the obsession, with the help of inside experts, others are hiring external consultants for this purpose. The naïve and not so experienced unexposed to the implication of this practice, feel that perhaps the benefits of liberalization can be obtained and challenge of internal and external competition met only through restructuring the organization. Others fully aware of the meaning of restructuring are doing so mainly to remove layers in the managerial hierarchy and cut down non-productive manpower on the plea of remaining lean, healthy and responsive to the market and competitive forces. A mix of motives thus impels them to take shelter under the magic word–restructuring. Whatever be the purpose or intention of the corporate actions, the fact remains that the underlying belief in restructuring is due to its potential to throw up redundancies in the managerial cadres and workers' ranks, as has been witnessed in many corporations in the USA, Europe and other advanced countries. Initially, an exercise in the area of organization planning and design takes into consideration the various criteria like the objectives to be achieved, the nature of business, i.e. trading, marketing, manufacturing or servicing, the place or the territory where business operations are to be conducted, the purpose to be attained, the people to be organized in a network of relationships, the product, the process, the technology to be adopted, the time dimension of operations and activities, the extent of mechanization, automation and computerization to be incorporated in the operational areas, the scope of interaction with the outside world at various points in an organization, i.e.

the competitors, customers suppliers, contractors, consultants, professionals, government agencies, the stockbrokers, the collaborators and the financial institutions—both banking and para-banking, as also other providers of capital such as NRIs, IMF and foreign partners and various other stakeholders.

Organic Aspect

Both mechanistic and organic aspects are taken into reckoning to design the structure. At worker-level after ascertaining the manning points in the context of machines and equipment to be operated, the process of operation to be adopted–both process or assembly line, or a combination of the two in requisite proportions and identifying the nature of activity skilled, semi-skilled, or unskilled, as also the mix of skills required to be incorporated in the activity stream and crew composition to be adopted to handle certain operations necessitating group interaction as well as work design, job distribution, input-output nexus and sequence of operations in work flow in consonance with the plant or factory layout, manning tables are worked out. Designations and titles whether job-oriented, hierarchy determined or directed by the nature and type of supervision at operating levels are then designed. Adequate care is bestowed on status, ego, anti socially determined practices and norms of the constituents. Such an elaborate and in-depth exercise preceding the process of organization structuring and arriving at numbers at the initial stages or even subsequently at different intervals is often given short shrift by a lopsided approach to the process of restructuring. Inside consultants or professionals associated with the exercise of restructuring may still be in a position to follow a logical, systematic and steady course and thus studiously scrutinize the impact of delayering, downsizing and consequently throwing up of redundancies. They can recommend certain interventions like upgradation of the manpower system through relevant skills related to behaviour or general management training and development programmes to re-deploy workers and managers on various jobs likely to be created due to expanded scope of business in the context of future growth in a related line of business or some other products sharing the same inputs like raw materials and technology. However, these may demand customized approach towards the end or, some entirely new areas, products or processes necessitating different or advanced technology leading perhaps to diversification sooner or later.

In such situations, restructuring may obviate the need to throw up redundancies and hopefully offer an opportunity to the enterprise to renovate, modernize and upgrade its manpower and associated systems. It can earn dividends in terms of employee dedication, involvement and consequently a higher level of productivity, which ultimately would have a salutary impact on the morale, motivation and well-being of the employees, managers and enterprise as a whole. In other situations, top management or the entrepreneurs Pressurize the manpower planners to identify surpluses in manpower whether at managerial, executive or at worker level just to satisfy their urge or ego for being termed as effective cost cutters. Or they are identified as industry leaders for being able to operate low ratios in terms of wage cost as percentage of sales turnover, productivity per man in terms of output input ratio or some other similar criterion.

Rule of Thumb

In certain other situations, where recourse to rule of thumb methods or unsystematic approach or any other compulsive factors like statutory obligations or even social responsibility to generate jobs, as has been often the case with PSUs in the early stages where redundant manpower does pose a grave problem to the very survival of an enterprise and business, recourse to downsizing or rationalization of manpower becomes a vital imperative, one should not hesitate to restructure, streamline and stay lean, mean (not lame) and responsive to the market impulses and challenges. This is essential as the wage burden of redundant and unproductive manpower could be substantial. Besides, escalation in wages-doubling almost every six to seven years-owing to longevity addition of regular annual increments (mostly unearned) and wage revisions could produce a crippling effect on the profitability of an enterprise. Perhaps, in such compulsive situations the various humanitarian approaches like counselling the parting employees, helping them with good references for alternative employment or even writing resumes and job search in addition to providing liberal severance financial compensation could assuage the hurt feelings of the erstwhile loyal and dedicated members of the organization. These measures would help to ameliorate the damage done to the self ego and thus far entrenched belief in the lifelong employment in the enterprise. It may also relieve to some extent the agony which a fired or separated employee undergoes due to sudden loss of job (loss of job is almost next to death in terms of pain it inflicts on the affected person) or fear of relocation, loss of status for self and family and the general feeling of malaise about self-worthlessness.

Family Enterprises

In the case of family-owned or private enterprises, consultants were often hired to recommend elimination or exile of certain inconvenient individuals or whistle blowers on the basis of some pseudo study in line with the brief handed out before assigning the contract. Of late, candid discussion precedes the engaging of consultants about the likely result this would produce in terms of redundancy in the managerial, executive and worker categories. The intention of the top management or proprietors being to reinforce their gut feeling and arm them with a tool to browbeat and convince the recalcitrant managers at the performing levels, who have to bear the brunt of reduced manpower resources either for the same or enhanced quantum of production.

It may so happen that an enterprise which has earlier faced a situation of delayering and downsizing of human resources on account of certain corporate changes like mergers, acquisitions, takeovers, asset stripping, divestitures, leveraged buyouts or some financial manipulations (showing sustained losses and grim prospects of recovery) with all the adverse consequences on the morale and sense of security of the surviving employees, yet another onslaught on them may completely cripple them and leave them breathless.

Obviously, the performance of the survivors would take a dip as perpetual fear of their being chopped off may render them morally bereft and lame. Whatever ambitions and aspirations they had harboured about their career growth and ultimate prospects in the corporation would have been frustrated and created a serious crisis in their lives. Another serious consequence could be the permanent exit of the elderly employees from the job market, a long period of search for a new job for the younger people (injured mice) with consequent burden on the limited resources of an individual and a strain on the family and society.

Entrepreneur's Education

Considering the undesirable outcome of this nefarious phenomenon of so-called restructuring, it is incumbent on the part of the manpower planners, HRD practitioners and management consultants to set in motion the process of education of the entrepreneurs, proprietors and top management who have the requisite powers and authority to checkmate this unhealthy practice of unsystematic and unscientific approach to the whole process of streamlining the organizational structure to face the challenge of change and competition within the country and abroad, and take recourse to a well-thought out process of in-depth, systematic and scientific study considering the following vital factors:

i) To establish the need for restructuring on the basis of some broad macro-level economic and financial indicators pointing the trend and direction of business and the enterprise vis-à-vis other entities engaged in similar or related activities.

ii) The perceived impact or actual effect of some recent

exercise in this direction as a result of merger, acquisition or a takeover of the enterprise.

iii) The likely impact of government policy on the present and near future status of business may be, due to demolition of protective barriers, withdrawal of incentives and encouragement of foreign capital in flow, investment and competition. Also provision of certain incentives to expand the activity within the country or across the national frontiers. Provision of government subsidy or such similar assistance to the employees rendered surplus, in the shape of social safety net, renewal fund or, certain specific facilities made available for retraining and re-deployment of the employees.

iv) Perceived ability or inability of the existing structure and its components to meet the requirements of the enterprise in the near future or in the next five years or so.

v) Other stray signals or specific technology-related changes or innovations or breakthroughs which might render the extant structure inadequate and inflexible to absorb the impact of such developments.

vi) The likely intent of business to expand by diversification, entering into collaboration or a joint venture for pushing up turnover either by increasing market share in the home market or taking recourse to exports in their existing product-line or new products in the existing foreign market or new markets.

vii) A broad profile of the available manpower resources in terms of education, training, professional preparation and expertise to handle new technology, process, product and the need to induct certain people in the critical areas and replace the ones who do not match with the altered job profile.

Need for Detailed Study

Based on the consideration of these and other related aspects it would be necessary to undertake detailed studies in respect of the following :

i) An analysis of the business trend and potential and the corporate plan (if any drawn up by the enterprise) and status of manpower in terms of levels, numbers, skill composition, age profile, sex ratio, sources of intake, induction, training and placement as also subsequent developmental and growth practices and processes to update and upgrade the manpower system.

ii) A study of the design of the organization structure and its mechanistic and organic features which render it viable or unviable in the context of latest concepts relating to human behaviour and improve intense interaction through group working, effective communication system, delegation, empowerment, participation, idea generation, innovation and creativity, decision-making, responsibility shouldering and rotating leadership role. A further problem into the process of group formation, task forces and networking to ascertain and assess the flexibility and responsiveness of the organization to the manifest and hidden needs of the customers and the market. Also its capacity to compete and collaborate with the competitors at the strategic levels and stay result-oriented and productive.

iii) To continue to provide exposure and keep educating the relevant authorities on a continuing basis during the course of the study, to control their impatience about the time-consuming process of study as also their anxiety to get immediate results from the study without incurring much cost. Experience indicates that while PSUs and large private undertakings engage various professionals in the field of HRD Industrial Engineering and manpower planning on their paid employment on a regular basis, small or even medium size enterprises varying in turnover even upto 15 to 20 crores feel hesitant to engage consultants for more than a few months. Some even expect the whole exercise of re-designing the structure and assess manpower requirement, as also streamline the systems within a month or so.

iv) The relayering exercise might lay stress on the responsibility aspect and effective utilization of executive recourses by avoiding one-to-one relationship and overlapping of roles. It may also incorporate the developmental aspect in the structure through stretching them mentally and physically and exposing to challenging opportunity to contribute visibly and boldly through their actions, executions and making decisions for future actions by their colleagues and subordinates. The executives must also be provided an opportunity to improve their potential for growth through proper job rotation in allied areas of activity and other roles requiring similar executive inputs

v) The assessment of numbers at executive levels must necessarily precede the use of various concepts and techniques of Industrial Engineering and organization design with suitable orientation and relevance to the need of an enterprise.

vi) At worker-level, a study of shop layout, sequence of operations, flow of work and materials, capacity of machines and their versatility, effective loading and utilization as also the process of production, the time dimension of operations like single shift, double shift and three shift working, the utilization of existing manpower, their crew composition in terms of skill mix and load sharing and supervisory practices to educate, guide and assist workers in improving productivity, maintain quality standards, through proper maintenance of their machines and tools and their own morale and motivation, needs to be carried out. Adequate allowances need to be provided to the workers to interact and socialize as also to cross fertilize their ideas with the co-workers to bring about improvement in their area of activity. Perhaps the Japanese practices of Kaizan should be given due consideration and adequate encouragement and time provided for such interventions.

vii) While assessing numbers, due provision must be made for future increase in work load and upsizing as other wise loss of trained manpower on the basis of existing load may create a problem in the future. In fact, with the declining trend of wage cost as a percentage of output in most of the manufacturing operations, it may prove counter-productive to reduce the wage bill further at the cost of highly capital intensive automation driven operations and processes.

However, even when it becomes evident that a certain number of people are redundant in the context of the present and future job load and restructuring, it is essential that a detailed and objective study is carried out further to ensure that the individual personality and job profile is adequately examined to arrive at a decision to relocate, retrench or retire certain employees. While adequate financial support with richly textured packages could be provided to all those who seek VR, others too are given due consideration. Besides, they could perhaps be provided moral and fiscal support in finding alternative jobs and relocating their families.

As for the survivors, there is need to boost their morale and allay the sense of insecurity for meeting a similar fate in the next move for restructuring. In fact, demoralized and insecure manpower gets frozen and the level of productivity dips irretrievably. Various palliatives like training, extra delegation, empowerment, liberal perks and other incentives do not really work when the "Damocles Sword" keeps hanging over their heads and their necks could be guillotined any time unexpectedly. This is more so in low union density areas both for unionized and un-unionized cadres.

In view of the foregoing discussion, it is essential that any exercise in regard to corporate restructuring is done considering the overall interest of the employees losing jobs instantly and even put on recall rosters, the survivors, the society and the enterprise itself. Virtually, restructuring is a tight rope walking and the anticipated benefits could sometimes lead to unexpected implications and a grievous loss to the organization.

CHAPTER – 2

Benchmarking: A Corporate Mona Lisa

Leonardo da Vinci, an Italian artist's unfinished portrait of Mona Lisa drawn some time between 1500 and 1506 became an ideal portrait in which features and symbolic over-tones of the person painted achieved a complete synthesis. This portrait was subsequently reproduced sixteen times mostly by his students each one claiming that the portrait made by him was the original and represented an ideal picture. Obviously, a painting of this nature where an effort was made to bring out the best features of the human form would excel every other living being in beauty and perfection. Perhaps, the corporate world or at least, the academicians, well-versed in the science of management mostly in terms of theory, are making all possible efforts to work out a corporate configuration which is representative of the ultimate in corporate success and excellence. Some of the authors have even listed certain characteristics which could make a corporation surpass any other competing entity in terms of performance and excellence.

Waterman and Peter's book entitled *In Search of Excellence* discusses a number of factors which could enable an organization to achieve excellence. Likewise, depending on one's own perceptions and the operating experience of the various organizations in their respective countries such studies about successful corporation have also been brought out in England and India. Though most of the factors leading to excellence of a corporation are common, some aspects do differ depending on the cultural orientation of the countries and the management respectively.

While these studies highlight the extant features which make an organization achieve excellence, the concept of benchmarking represents a comparative study of the best-in-class companies on various dimensions like manufacturing, marketing or even general managerial practices. A book on the subject of benchmarking written by Robert C. Camp, an executive in Xerox Corporation brings out the concepts, techniques and processes of benchmarking in lucid terms. It also puts emphasis on some other factors which could assist in the process of using the techniques of benchmarking. Virtually benchmarking directs companies to focus outside their own walls and have the goals and the targets geared towards being the best in the world. Partly, benchmarking is the art of imitating and partly strategic alliance with other companies.

Benchmarking is, thus, a formal process of measuring and comparing a company's operations, products and services against those of the top competitors both within and outside with a company's primary industry. The aim of benchmarking is to identify the leading companies' secrets of success and to copy them where possible. It is also a process of gathering comparative data and also the underlying processes that produce the data, which help companies to achieve outstanding position in the market. In addition to gathering quantitative data, the qualitative information has also to be taken into reckoning for the purpose of benchmarking. While some of the companies may wish to compare their best performed functions with the strongest company in the field, yet others would like to take up their weak points and then make a comparative study with the strong companies.

Under the circumstances, benchmarkings benefits as a strategic planning method are that it identifies the keys to success for each area studied and provides specific quantitative targets as also creates awareness of the key managerial approaches and helps the various companies to cultivate a culture where change, adoption and continuous improvement are actively pursued. The underlying assumption being that the HRD aspect which enables a corporation to motivate its executives and staff in the philosophy of benchmarking and its techniques and processes is given due attention and emphasis in terms of information sharing goal setting and achievement of targets in the context of their organization's capabilities and strengths.

It may be pointed out that the various techniques and practices like inter-firm comparison, constant watching and monitoring of activities of the competitors, pirating the technologies and process of other companies; operations, baiting and attracting the experienced key executives and employees of other companies are some of the practices being followed in most companies. In fact, it is a normal phenomenon to go in for studies, surveys and investigations within the industry in which one is interested or even other companies handling different products and services. Some of the corporations, either intending to operate across the national frontiers or already operating on a global level keep watching the strategies and operating practices of other corporations on a continuing basis so as to be able to enhance the market share, reinforce their marketing muscle and even expand in some of the markets. Such studies mostly confine the scope of analysis to the marketing operations of the other companies as also the quality of products offered by them to the customer. Based on such studies, they chalk out their future strategies for doing business within the country and abroad.

Bearing this scenario in mind, it would be desirable to probe deeper into the concept and practice of benchmarking which is gaining wide popularity in most of the advanced countries of the world. For instance, while only a small percentage of the 'Fortune 500 companies had introduced the practice of benchmarking in 1985, the number of such companies has increased to beyond 50 per cent in recent years. It is difficult to say, how far these companies have been able to achieve the desired results, in their areas of operation, vis-à-vis their competitors. In fact, some of the best performing corporations who would have been benchmarked in the areas of human resource development or marketing like IBM are no longer as successful as they were some years ago. Perhaps, functional excellence or operational proficiency in the corporate context may be more a function of time and the market conditions relating to consumer taste, consumer preference and various other socio-cultural and economic factors.

Changes occurring in the areas of technology, economic conditions, social norms and other factors could result in making some of the practices either obsolete or less effective in course of time. The element of time itself and emergence of innovative practices in the areas of production, marketing strategy, HRD and financial fields may result in discarding some of the best techniques and practices being followed by some of the companies. For example, the emergence, of the small sector and the mushrooming of a number of tiny and small enterprises which are lean in structure and highly responsive to the market impulses have overtaken some of the largest global corporations in terms of performance and growth. These small units prefer to cling to their field of expertise in management, production, marketing or distribution and collaborate with other units for mutual help and support in terms of information sharing, supply of inputs (spares, components and sub-assemblies) marketing, distribution and even training and development of their executives and operatives. They, therefore, do not have to benchmark other companies' operations and practices as a part of management strategy. Rather, each unit thrives on others' expertise in their area of operation.

Some of the latest practices relating to marketing like that of franchising in the retail business have made the earlier all pervasive marketing networks obsolete and redundant. Some of the studies like the one conducted by Waterman and Peters and discussed in their book *In Search of Excellence* lay emphasis on the aspect of "stick to the knitting" which means that one must concentrate on one's areas of expertise and specialization rather than go in for the best techniques and practices followed by the competitors or other organizations in their field of activity. Each industry, may be steel, cement, coal, paper, textile jute and heavy machinery manufacturing industry have their own techniques and technologies for value addition and conversion and turning out the final product. Besides, the way such enterprises are organized and evolve systems, procedures and controls in terms of the day-to-day operations, communication and actual working practices would vary to a great extent. May be, the financial policy and practices being followed in the coal industry are not suitable for the steel industry. Likewise, the functional composition, organizational design and the financial practices for handling funds, credit policies and cash flow represent a different regime than the one followed in the paper industry.

Perhaps, gathering of data and information about the best quantitative and qualitative techniques and practices being followed in successful enterprises may not really result in a combination of the best techniques and practices to be adopted and followed by the benchmarking enterprises and could perhaps result in a mismatch between different components of the organization. Organizational balance may also be disturbed. Therefore, the pursuit of excellence through benchmarking may prove to be a mirage and may not really yield the desired results. On the other hand, the combination of these techniques and practices may lead to a peculiar type of configuration in terms of organization design, communication system and the managerial practices. It may also not result in higher efficiency and productivity or better product features in terms of quality and end use. For instance, Tata's organizational philosophy of providing full autonomy to the various enterprises in diverse fields under its fold, which has worked remarkably well thus far and was a point of envy for other companies in India, has now turned out to be a major threat to the very survival of the Tata empire.

Obviously, a corporate portrait drawing on the basis of benchmarking of others' philosophy, policies, techniques, processes and operating practices may not create a corporate Mona Lisa. Possibly, the whole exercise may end up in a ridiculously disproportionate corporate portrait.

CHAPTER – 3

Changing Corporate Perspective : Value Addition Down the Line

The last few decades have witnessed a continuous innovation in determining as to what really happens in the process of manufacturing and production of goods and services. At some stage, production was reckoned as the process of manufacturing a product by following certain steps or activities manually or mechanically under different sub-processes and assembled at various stages to have the final product. The various items could be produced either internally within the factory or some of the items could be out-sourced and finally assembled along with the internally produced items.

Over time, a study into the total process of manufacturing lead to the conceptualization of a new phenomenon termed as conversion. While the main conversion activity was supposed to be performed in the factory premises of the producer of the final product, some of the activities at the vendors' level also involved the conversion techniques. These activities could have been performed either when converting a raw material into an input fed to the main manufacturer or when assembling parts of a sub-assembly for the buyer.

This particular concept of denoting production held sway for quite some time. And the role of the various actors was recognized to some extent while reserving the final act for the manufacturer of the end product. Negotiations for entering into supply contracts with the vendors revolved around the terms of the contract relating to quality, price, lead time, mode of delivery and credit or cash arrangement. The social dimension of the whole affair was thus conspicuously absent and the relationship was oriented commercially in a cut and dried form. Vendors could be dropped from the list of main buyers depending on the discretion and convenience of the latter.

Value Addition

Of late, the concept of value addition has gained currency in the industrial world. Whether one is engaged in production, supply of inputs, marketing or trading, provision of various services like information, know-how, consultancy, engineering, transportation, warehousing and retailing, one can legitimately claim his contribution to the value addition of the product at various stages of transition from the conceptual stage to the final stage of delivery to the end user.

This phenomenon thus gets mainifested in positioning of the activities of the various actors along the range of value addition. On the whole, continuous value enhancement whether in conceptual terms or the physical sense gets effectuated in different ways. While abstract thinking, dreaming or star gazing might aid conceptualization to a great extent, the practical people associated with the physical activity get their ideas from their actions and make an endeavour to translate these ideas into value adding actions. The cycle thus goes on.

However, certain factors which are glaringly absent in the entire gamut of activity of the various actors are the roles, relationships and interactions, which, while integrated, could lead to re-invention of values. The latest research in the area of manufacturing, production and services reveals that there is a need for systematic social innovation and constant designing and redesigning of the business system.

Reinventing Values

In fact, based on changes in the social spheres there is a need to re-invent values and reconfigurate roles and relationships amongst the various agents like customers, suppliers, partners and business allies. Virtually, the activities would need to be reshuffled among the various actors and matched with their roles for better value enhancement. Since the customer is the end user of the various offerings (products/services involving activities-integrated or not-at the level of various actors) it is essential that the customer is made to participate in the process of value creation of the product, process or service. Sharing of know-how and technology involved in such processes, which can even be performed by the customer at his premises such as assembly of certain components (supplied at low cost) to get the final product say, furniture items, white products and other durables. Semi-processed food items could also be reckoned in this category. In fact, competencies of a particular enterprise could be matched with the customers and participation ensured in the value addition process. This practice would not only lead to effective and efficient working of a product but would also result in after sale service and maintenance of the item at much lower cost and effort on the part of the supplier and the user.

There is also a need to appreciate the roles and inter-relationships of the various vendors of a firm.

Sharing Expertise

Sharing of expertise and knowledge of technology of out-sourced items with the vendor could lead to better control on quality and operational reliance of the items supplied by the latter. This approach may as well entail repositioning of the activities of the vendors along the value addition range vis-à-vis their earlier regime of operation.

So as to share expertise, integrate and re-invent the value enhancing process through closer participation of the customer, proper development of network of facilities would be a vital imperative. At the minimum, a customer expects easy access to the factory, showroom or sale point of a firm. A customer would also appreciate having drive in facility and appropriate space for parking his vehicle. These facilities are glaringly absent in metropolises like Delhi, Mumbai and Kolkata.

Paradox

Paradoxically, business ethics and organizational value systems imposed on a low basal moral societal structure and abysmally poor political standards of the politicians surviving on money, muscle and gunpower betray all sincere efforts to upgrade the business and commercial practices. Under the circumstances, some of the following aspects would need to be considered.

1) Whether the system of value addition and concept of reinventing values for the various offerings (products and services) could be practised and preached notwithstanding social and political conditions, when the whole emphasis has to be on a sincere and honest approach to the relationship between industry and its vendors, contractors and regulatory bodies. The roles of the various actors too have to be recast and matched with the competencies of the producers of the final product.

2) Would the concept of reinventing values for the final offerings to the customer whose participation is considered paramount in the whole scheme of things have any meaning for the players in the tiny and small informal sectors in the metropolis who usually take pride in peddling spurious and sub-standard products? Cheating the customer and extortion are the rampant practices and norms.

3) In the prevalent market situation where even experienced executives with long standing in business and industry shudder to think of entering a shop or a showroom owing to the fear of being robbed of their wallets and fobbed off with some faulty or substandard item. The concept of customer participation in the creation of value to the product seems utopian.

Client Education

However, there is a ray of hope in this dismal scenario, especially when one views the situation in the context of the formal business sector. Here, a large number of professionals from various disciplines, bound by their codes of conduct and mental make up, could play a positive role in promoting ethical practices and ensuring customer and vendor participation. They can thus mobilize value creation in their clients.

The necessary prerequisite would be a gradual and involved process of education of the various actors within the enterprise and outside. Regulatory bodies too would need to be educated and persuaded to stick to the standards of quality and specifications prescribed while inspecting and clearing the various products from the factories and showrooms, rather than violating the norms and bending the rules by indulging in rapacious practices.

CHAPTER - 4

Corporate Ethics : A Gripping Dilemma

Recently the corporate world seems to have been seized by a vexed dilemma over the question of ethics in various countries around the globe. While India has been witnessing a number of scandals, frauds and scams in the banking companies, stock market and the business enterprises for quite some time, the world's super industrial powers like the USA, Japan and Germany are now passing through a critical phase in this regard. The mal practices relate to expense accounts, commissions, diversion of funds, manipulation of the revenue line, over invoicing, under invoicing and myriad other accounting irregularities. Unravelling of Enron Corp, Arthur Andersen, World Com, Adelphia, Merrillynch, Deutsche, Telcom AC, Tyco and Xerox (India) have virtually given a rude shock to the regulatory authorities, other controlling powers and the community at large.

On top of all these scams, the various cases involving huge bribes and kickbacks like Watergate and Aero Space in the USA and Bofors and defence procurements in India have revived memories of even Dharma Teja scandal (shipping magnate) of yesteryears. Besides, stock market scams perpetrated by Lt. Harshad Mehta, Ketan Shah and others have also caused considerable concern and anxiety to the controlling powers, the business community and other stakeholders. Small investors are thus thoroughly baffled.

In the normal course of business activity, the corporates have to deal with the various agencies having profound ethical implications at every point of interaction. Their plight and consternation could be judged further by the perceptions and observations of the various philosophers, ideologues, economists and statesmen. According to Galbraith, entrepreneurs are to pursue objectives which are rational and purely economic and it is the regulatory nature of law and the political process-rather than the invisible hand of the market place-sthat would turn these objectives to the common good. Good paster and Matthews aver that the system is expected to provide the moral direction and the moral responsibility of business is confined to political and legal obedience. Thus they locate morality, ethics, responsibility and conscience in the system of rules and incentives.

Johan Ladd believes that "we can't and must not expect formal organizations to be honest, courageous, considerate, sympathetic or to have moral integrity." But Peter Drucker advocates the moral responsibility of business, in a society of organizations like ours, where the social well-being of individuals is affected by the conduct and sincerity of large enterprises. He thus contradicts other philosophers and statesmen and believes that their outlook and thesis could prove disastrous for the modern society.

Other constraints as imposed by the various constituencies could be stated as:

Politicians : Democracy is a political institution which survives mainly on the principle of give and take. Hence the corporates who often render financial support and voters who help during electioneering, expect certain gains from the politicians in times of need. Those holding ministerial portfolios and other important positions take huge sums of money in return for such favours. This practice was more rampant during the licence raj days in India. To generate money on a large scale the corporates have to take recourse to certain undesirable and unethical means. This, therefore, poses a serious constraint to the CEOs and other senior executives.

Bureaucracy : It is very well known that at every level and in every department of the government, State or Central, the common man, the trader and the business community have to bribe the various officers including peons. The file or the paper does not move without speed money. In a situation like this, the common man is forced to succumb to unethical practices.

Money Providers : People handling vast reservoirs of funds misuse their powers while lending money to the business community. A certain percentage of funds advanced to entrepreneurs usurped by the managers is considered a normal practice. Under such circumstances, corporates dealing with the financial institutions and banks have to follow the dictates of the lenders rather than sticking to their morals.

Corporate Accounting : It was a normal assumption that the accounting principles, procedures and standards evolved by USA were foolproof and could protect the veracity of the accounting statements, the balance sheet and the profit and loss account compiled by the chartered accountants and audited by the auditors. Yet, recent corporate frauds in the case of Enron, World Com and others have led to the belief that it is not only the viability of the system but also the character or self-imposed discipline of the various agencies who have to work the system. No doubt, a couple of heads including those of the CEOs and Directors may play a role in the process. Punitive measures may also help the situation to a limited extent as, even with stern penalties it has not been possible to eliminate crime, violence, murders and various frauds from the society anywhere in the world.

Stakeholders' Expectations : Even such CEOs who have been performing exceedingly well for quite some time fall prey to the vacuities of the market and yield to the temptation of by passing the rules. In spite of this, when the corporates do not perform to the expectations of the stakeholders, the CEOs and other senior executives take recourse to unethical practices.

Individual Greed : In the materialistic society where the status of an individual is gauged by the volume of money accumulated by him, the individual becomes a victim to the temptation of acquiring wealth by any means. Social comparison with other corporates or the CEOs plays no less a role in influencing the mind of the individual to make money by hook or crook. The morals and the ethics preached by the religion, the social institutions, the business schools and the family are forgotten when the individual is overwhelmed by the lure of wealth.

It is, therefore, doubtful whether shareholder activism and sweeping powers vested in regulatory bodies could abate unethical practices in business organizations by CEOs and others who are part of the larger society plagued by pervasive greed and corruption. Current popular report may, however, prove to be a temporary deterrent.

CHAPTER – 5

Corporate Social Responsibility : An Ever Growing Need

The concept of social service is almost as old as mankind. The underlying spirit for social welfare is the care of the needy. The earliest encounter the writer of this piece had, was in Pakistan at Sargodha during the mid-40s of the last century. The various religious institutions like Sanatan Dharm, Arya Samaj and gurudwara had organized welfare bodies for the depressed and deprived sections of the society. A few prominent institutions like widow homes, orphanages, homes for the handicapped, dharamshalas, community halls, educational institutions and so on were the manifestations of the community service rendered by the various religious bodies. Later on, at the time of partition of the country in 1947, the process of social service was witnessed even in greater measures after the vast populace migrated to India from Pakistan. The huge mass of humanity residing in refugee camps were offered help and service in the shape of medical facilities, food, ration items, clothes, shelter and so on by the various social, religious and business organizations.

Even though the number of business houses was small, yet most of them according to their mission, commitment, and contemporary values had organized various kinds of services through their trusts, foundations and charitable institutions. Establishment of schools, colleges, vocational and professional centres, construction and maintenance of temples, gurudwaras and even masjids by the leading business houses were found in fairly large numbers in different parts of the country. Also pressed into service of the society were the various scientific and research bodies established, run and maintained by these houses.

Yet, considering the size of the population, growing

number of destitutes, swelling ranks of the unemployed and people below the poverty line, creation of huge slums in and around the metropolis, ever growing migrant population from the villages to the cities, lack of resources for their upkeep and the basic necessities such as food, shelter and clothing have aggravated the need for community service and welfare activities further.

The scope of activity for the corporates in the area of social responsibility has thus become multi-dimensional. Usually, corporates cater to the welfare needs of four different constituencies like employees, stakeholders, general public and ruralites in various ways. Provision of high quality products and services at a reasonable price is the paramount social responsibility of the modern corporates in addition to the provision of social services. To gauge compliance, some corporates have even introduced social audit sumoto. For instance, most of the public sector undertakings and private sector enterprises which had either come up during the 1950s, and 1960s or, the ones coming up now in the green fields had developed captive townships, hospitals, community centres, schools and colleges and playgrounds for the welfare of their employees. Besides, they had also extended help to the supporting and surrounding population, in the shape of small-scale cottage industries for providing inputs to the main production units. Other facilities like training centres for tailoring, glove-making, basket-making, knitting and weaving were also offered to the women, especially widows. Ancillary units too had been organized on commercial lines to rehabilitate the population displaced by the various factories and plants.

However, one issue which has been constantly pricking the conscience of the mission-oriented corporations is the extension of the various developmental activities to the rural sector. The various PSUs like SAIL, CIL, BHEL, ONGC and private business houses like Tatas, Birlas, Thapars, Modis, Singhanias, Escorts, Reliance and so on have been endeavouring to extend medical facilities, educational facilities and coaching for sports and athletics in the rural areas. Even recreation events are being organized in the village areas for the entertainment of the people. Most of the activities, particularly in PSUs were undertaken in the initial stages on the basis of comprehensive surveys and studies. Both PSUs and business houses made budgetary provisions for the community services in their annual plans. Incidentally, TISCO had envisaged a five-year budgetary provision for the various activities to be taken up in the nearby villages in the late 1970s. Likewise, SAIL too had drawn up a specific time-bound plan in this regard.

For instance, one of the biggest units of SAIL, i.e. Bokaro Steel had conducted a detailed survey in the Kiriburu and Maghatuburu iron mines in the tribal areas of Bihar and Orissa. The door-to-door survey focused on the existing status of various facilities, namely drinking water, irrigation, education, medical, facilities, roads, post offices, handloom weaving, vocational training, goatry and poultry projects. Based on findings, the socio-economic development plan was envisaged keeping in view the cultural mores, mental barriers, social inhibitions vocational stigma, aptitude of the people and natural bestowment and limitations of the region. Since involvement of the people of the area was considered extremely important, the local agencies like the village-level leaders, elders, local youth, school teachers, mukhias, BDOs, union leaders and the local survey department were consulted and involved in the process. Obviously, a need was felt for the various facilities in the tribal areas. Perhaps, in the absence of a detailed survey it would have been difficult to pinpoint specific areas for development.

In advanced countries like the US, the emphasis has shifted from unorganized and scattered social welfare activities to well-organized, well-financed and well-managed non-profit organizations. These entities operate with the help of regular staff, volunteers and the board of directors. One unique feature of the non-profits is that they have to operate in the absence of a visible financial measure like the 'bottomline', which, parameter, is usually available to the corporates in their commercial endeavours. The non-profits operate on the basic mission of changing the style of life and the attitude of a man. In fact, these institutions are performing the role of change agents. To illustrate, these social institutions organize special rehabilitation programmes for the drug addicts, socially discarded, mentally retarded, socially uprooted and depressed people. According to US estimates, employees numbered nearly 8 million and volunteers 80 million who were actively involved in social and community service projects in the 1990s. However, measured in terms of percentage of GNP the figure was abysmally small. This holds good for other countries as well.

Considering the bulging population of the slums in India and general level of deprivation, corporate as well as other non-profit institutions need to accelerate their activities.

It has been revealed in a recently conducted poll by Tata Energy Research Institution, that MNCs are not really conscious of their social responsibility. In fact, people expect a lot more from them in the various areas of community service as also de-escalation of their activities with regard to production and marketing of various products like tobacco, alcoholic beverages, mining, chemicals and so on. The minimum that the public expects from the MNCs is that they must take necessary steps to eliminate the adverse effect of their activity on human life and avarice. Besides, they should also reduce the depletion of natural resources. Further, international bodies like Rotary Club, Lions Club, the Red Cross, Scouts' guilds and other non-profits too need to accelerate their activities in this sphere, especially in the event of natural calamities, famines, riots, war, epidemics and major accidents.

Virtually, there is a tremendous scope for social service both for individuals and the institutions.

CHAPTER - 6

The Political-Corporate Nexus

Politicians and businessmen make strange bedfellows. The relationship between the two is purely materialistic and matter of fact. While the politicians seek links with business for mercenary support, businessmen endeavour to come closer to the politicians to gain favour for all such issues which help them to promote their business interest. The nexus between the two entities is rather tenuous and ephemeral unless a particular individual aspires to gain prominence and visibility in the business world and society to attain the status of a celebrity. Big business houses of India like the Tatas, Birlas, Thapars, Singhania and Reliance are known for producing such individuals who have attained national identity. Some of them have become known even in international business circles. Such entrepreneurs and managers create business inner circles and class-wise networks to lobby and influence the thinking of politicians to enact business-related legislation and evolve policy frameworks which help the former to safeguard, promote and enhance their business objectives. In the process, the policies, regulatory framework, the control mechanism and guidelines developed by the political powers have a pervasive effect on the whole gamut of business activity. This being the external environmental influence and control on the corporate world, any change in the political complexion, structure or the collaborative framework of the political set up is likely to have considerable impact on the organization structure, policies, procedures and operating practices of the business enterprises. The extent of the impact would depend on the degree of change. When the change is sudden and of a massive nature the impact could be quite unsettling initially. At times it could create tremors and cause ripples across the length and breadth of the corporate world. Major upheavals could virtually cause a sort of earthquake in realms of business and have a much wider and pervasive effect. The politicians and governments which have been simply maintaining a status quo or, virtually following a laissez faire approach would not cause much disturbance to the business people in the event of their being uprooted. However, the government and the politicians who have been able to initiate major policy measures or have set in motion a new regime either liberal or conservative and control-oriented, would naturally give either a big push to business activity or put an embargo on the ongoing activity.

Contract Areas

Yet another factor which influences the nature and extent of change in corporate activity is the area of contact of the business with the politicians at different levels of hierarchy. Some organizations endeavour to develop level-by-level contact with the political hierarchy through their own organizational structure at the local, state and national level. In a situation like this, wherever, a change is perpetrated at various contact points owing to the uprooting of the party president at the local level, a sort of upheaval is created in the political world and consequently the corporate world. This necessitates a fresh bout of intense thinking and activity in the corporate realms.

Besides keeping a close watch on the changing situation, and identifying the likely successor politicians, the business executive would even take recourse to intense lobbying to develop contacts with the new actors. They have to study the whole situation carefully and understand the political leanings of the new players. Some of the politicians might have conservative or liberal views on business, while others may maintain a neutral stance.

Impact Points

Such an uncertainty about the likely pattern of behaviour and leanings of the politicians could impel the corporate executive to keep a close watch on some of the following areas :

i) Sudden impact on the value of the stock of the company and the overall trend in the share market.

ii) Impact on the various policy initiatives taken by the previous government and the changes likely to occur in the policy regime.

iii) Likely change in the volume of production, expansion plans, trade volumes, direction of foreign trade, diversification plans, investment policy, price structure (due to change in excise, customs, taxes), credit vs equity plans, financial structure, capitalization plans and interaction with the financial and non-financial institutions.

iv) Loss of business in the event of liberalization of imports, especially for protected and monopoly items.

v) Freedom or restraint on entering into joint ventures, collaboration, franchising arrangements with foreign business enterprises as also putting up of production facilities in other countries and the quantum of investment required in such ventures.

vi) Nature, range, volume and direction of exports as also the level of imports of various types of items, plant, machinery and equipment.

vii) Availability of free foreign exchange for undertaking imports as also boosting exports related to plans, programmes and activity.

viii) Types of organization structure, levels in the hierarchy, job titles, experience levels as also place of posting of the various executives assigned liaison and coordination responsibility with the government functionaries and politicians.

ix) Impact on HRD and manpower policies and programmes in terms of employment, quotas recruitment and placement training, retraining and redeployment, redundancies, retrenchment, voluntary separations, social benefits, welfare measures and various wage-related policies.

x) Deployment of foreign nationals from the collaborating organizations, their tenure, emoluments and other service conditions.

xi) Training of Indian executives abroad and the necessary release of foreign exchange.

The list could be lengthened further, if a detailed scrutiny is done about the areas of impact at the micro-level within the various segments and sub-systems of enterprises. Suffice to say, that the greater the political upheaval (like the one in USSR), the deeper, more pervasive and intense would be the impact in the corporate world.

Counteraction

However, the redeeming feature of this whole cataclysmic phenomenon would be as to how the managers and entrepreneurs tackle the situation and manage their business affairs without getting bruised unduly.

Given the democratic form of governmental system and 'give and take' as the sine-qua non for existence and survival of the two main entities, i.e. business and politicians, some of the following measures could be considered to arrive at a compromise position to mitigate or at least minimize the perilous effect of political upheavals.

i) Managers and entrepreneurs develop a certain reliable sensory mechanism to be able to scan the political environment on a continuing basis and be in a position to visualize the trends.

ii) While adhering to their basic values and ethics in the context of corporate mission and philosophy, to keep reviewing their strategy and approach in their field of activity where the boundaries of business and political system interface.

iii) Instead of initiating prompt action in response to a particular policy measure initiated by the government, watch the situation for some time. This may alleviate the position as often various interest groups pressurize the government to revise and review the various provisions and elements of a policy. Business lobbies could also influence the policy review process if they could not envisage such a policy initiative or could not participate in the process of policy formulation. Frequently hastily evolved anaemic policies and plans get revoked when adverse implications are pointed out.

iv) Managers could maintain close contacts with the various institutions like chambers, federations, associations and other bodies who normally represent and espouse business causes and concerns.

v) On the slightest indication of the declining fortunes of political bigwigs may keep close tabs on the situation and be in a position to realign their interactive strategy at the contact point.

vi) Managers may also try to maintain a rapport with the leaders of the large opposition parties who could be the likely contenders for the seats of power.

vii) Contingency plans appropriate to various areas of operation of business within and outside its boundaries could be drawn up and kept in a state of readiness.

Managers and executives could be educated to use these plans on the basis of mock or simulated studies.

viii) Virtually each and every manager has to be sensitized to the political system and its influence on the operations of business, systematic exposure to the elements of the political process which impact the fortunes of business should form part of the training and development programme of an enterprise.

ix) Managers could even educate their employees and other associates like suppliers, vendors, contractors, consultants, distributors, dealers, customers, shareholders and other stakeholders to avoid a partisan attitude with political bosses and be matter of fact in the their dealings and relationship.

CHAPTER - 7

Corporate Wars

The history of the corporate world is replete with internecine wars relating to their field of activity. Any enterprise which is engaged in the marketing and selling of a product or services or even engaged in the trading activity has been confronted with competition from the various sources. As a result of this, the corporate world has to take recourse to advertising either to create awareness or to remain visible to their clients and consumers and stay ahead of competition. Often these ads could take the form of hip pocket phrases, slogans or TV jingles. In the early days, when the TV had not come on the scene, slogans or catch phrases were displayed on banners, hoardings or even on walls. Posters with salacious pictures too were made use of, especially by garment designers. At times ad text was also peppered with interesting anecdotes.

There was a constant endeavour on the part of the companies to thwart competition or beat the rivals at their own game. Price wars, road shows, promotional gimmicks or various other tactics were made use of. The story was the same even for the top ranking multinationals spanning various continents of the world. For example, the MNCs in the oil world, namely Burmah Shell, ESSO and Caltex who were engaged in the marketing activity in India would often come out with slogans and catch phrases to attract or impress the customers. One of the earliest slogans used by Burmah Shell was "In India's life and every moving part of it" which was subsequently changed to "In India's life and part of it". Presumably this was done to obviate criticism from some quarters about its relevance. While this practice continued, some time around the late 1950s ESSO came out with a catch phrase which almost sent shock waves in the world of Shell across various continents. One fine morning, on every gas station a slogan "puts tiger in the tank" appeared everywhere at the same time and in the same style. Even the children were attracted by this slogan. A child once enquired from his father as to how the tiger went into the tank. On this, the child's father explained to him that the tiger got into the tank along with petrol through the nozzle of the tank. One day the child got hold of a toy tiger and put it in the nozzle of the tank of the car. Incidentally, such funny catch phrases were rather limited in number in those days. Whereas the situation has undergone a tremendous change these days.

For instance, Colas-both Coke and Pepsi-are coming out with peculiar catch phrases along with jingles which could misguide innocent people, especially the children. Instead of putting a tiger in the fuel tank of the car, the Colas are putting a tiger in the human body. No doubt either to get the bottle of Cola or after having imbibed Cola the individual starts jumping from mountain to mountain or from one vehicle to the other moving at a fast speed. At times, the character in the jingle makes an all out effort to grab a bottle of Cola encountering all possible hurdles and incalculable risks. The only apprehension is that the children may not take the ad in the real sense of the word seriously and get involved in misadventures.

Some of the funny phrases which are being used are as under :

"Yeh Dil Mange More" – Pepsi

"Life Ho To Aisi" – Coke.

"Jo Bhi Ho Jai Coca Cola Enjoy" – Coke.

It would not be a surprise, if the Colas mint out similar phrases in the near future and continue to browbeat each other. For instances, the Coke phrase regarding official drink was retorted to by Pepsi with the slogan, "There is nothing official about it" meaning thereby, that it was a drink of the masses. No doubt,

Coke executives would have been humbled by the ingenuity of Pepsi guys.

May be, some of the following phrases in sync with their ethos could be utilized by either of them in future with appropriate jingles :

1. Cola piyo aur jug jug jiyo.
2. Cola piyo aur jiyo mere lal.
3. Cola piyo aur jiyo.
4. Cola bolay bale bale.
5. Cola khola mere mann dola.

However, one thing which needs to be kept in mind is that both Colas have been struggling for quite some time to come out of the accounting minefield and reach break even point. Incidentally, both have been running at heavy losses so far. Perhaps, Coke has now hit this elusive corporate benchmark according to their own version. All the same, it may be interesting to know that Colas have no doubt become a part of life of the Indians-in fact, the nationals of the world. Colas provide a different type of value to diverse sections of society at various levels, such as entertainment, quenching thirst, beating the heat, ego satisfaction and so on. For the unscrupulous it is a God sent opportunity to push out fake drinks in Cola containers. It may be pointed out that even in day-to-day life, a guest or a friend coming to somebody's house usually expects Cola drinks in preference to other drinks-hot or cold. This is so at least with the younger population.

In the early days, when Colas, particularly Coca Cola made its appearance on the Indian territory, some of the following apprehensions were expressed :

1. Excessive intake of Coke could lead to cancer.

2. An overdose of sugar in the Cokes could cause diabetes and dental problems.

3. Regular use of Coke might transform people, especially children into addicts.

However, all these fears have been allayed in course of time owing to acquiescence of the Health Agencies of the various countries and indifference of the people to the propagation of such a risk.

CHAPTER - 8

Celebrity Endorsement

Corporates are sinking huge money on celebrity endorsement of their products, services and messages. Perhaps it would amount to asking too much of human nature to suggest that instead of going whole hog after others and following the calf path one might pause and think for a moment as to what impact such an act would have on one's scheme of things. Probably, in earlier days when the modes of communications were limited and most of the ads were displayed either in newspapers or carried through posters or even broadcast on radio. The process had the same impact on top of the mind recall for a limited segment of the target audience who were literate enough to read the papers or, other written material or, the ones who would care to remain glued to the radio at home or at the barber's shop or a paan shop. Perhaps this might have had a deep influence on the minds of the people who would accept a product on its face value in terms of usage and benefits depending on the version of the celebrities as, the level of credibility of the corporates like Tatas, Birlas, Singhanias and MNCs like ESSO, CALTEX and Burmah Shell and HLL was quite high in the public. In the initial stage, even social activities performed and community services offered by these business houses for the welfare of the society could have led to the success of such a practice. Also there was not much gap between the quality and benefit professed by the corporates and the actual perception held by the users.

However, over time, the position has undergone a major change and the gap between reality and claims has widened considerably. This might have been occasioned owing to some of the following factors:

1) The number of products and their substitutes has increased in geometrical proportion.

2) A large number of brands and sub-brands for the same product without much differentiation has appeared in the market.

3) Start ups with limited resources have brought out many products with sub-standard quality.

4) The number of enterprises has shot up considerably with the rise in population, nuclear family system, reducing dependence on family pastimes or vocations, mobility of population, spread of education, higher aspiration level and the urge for achievement through wealth creation and possession.

5) The change in mindset to be on one's own instead of banking on limited job opportunities in industry, government, agriculture and other related areas.

6) Entrepreneurial spirit generated by exposure to the situation in the developed countries where self-supporting vocations command status, dignity and wider acceptance in the social context.

7) Rising entry barriers encountered by local entrepreneurs from the MNCs and product dumping.

8) Overall competition in the market created by a mix of locals and MNCs.

9) General impression in the mind of corporates that celebrity endorsement not only creates product/brand awareness but also easy recall and credibility. As a consumer of various products, brands and services the author wishes to make the following submissions :

    i) Different segments of population, ethnic groups, communities, literates, illiterates, knowledgeable people, executives, professional and scientifically minded people react differently to celebrity endorsements.

ii) Cola companies suffering losses year after year or even Deawoo motors would need to realize that celebrity endorsements with massive pay outs do not really bring business and sell their products. Perhaps, Coke and Pepsi which are widely known the world over are doing more good to the celebrities than to themselves. In the case of Deawoo motors their bankruptcy in their own country has negated all efforts to sell their products through celebrities who earlier captured the market by dint of their corporate image and product quality endorsed by users as per the product experience delivered.

iii) Each individual views a celebrity from his own perspective in the context of his interest and environmental influence. This phenomenon is manifest in the interviews conducted usually by TV correspondents. Some time ago, in response to a question by a correspondent to a shoe polisher about who should be the Prime Minister of India, the later replied, 'Govinda, the film star would be the best candidate'. May be, God willing, Govinda some day in future joins politics and establishes his credentials for the job. But as it is, it appears incongruous and far-fetched. The point I am trying to make is that people may have a great regard for a particular celebrity but that does not mean that they would be persuaded to buy the brand or product endorsed by him. People usually form their own opinion and mostly go by the word of mouth about a particular product. This is applicable to all sorts of products which may be durables or consumer products. Housewives, don't ever buy a consumer durable or even a common item like a detergent unless they have consulted a large number of their contacts. Obviously corporate buyers themselves don't follow their own practice or advise their customers to go by the celebrity endorsement of the various products they procure as their inputs.

With due apology to the celebrities, I would like to caution the corporates to be careful about the way they advertise their products, brands or services. Let them focus on quality, service, and ethical practices.

Also creative sales promotion strategies may bring richer dividends.

CHAPTER – 9

Corporate Disclosure Conceals More Than It Reveals

Audit function has assumed great significance in the corporate governance process in the recent past. Virtually, multi layered audit structure has evolved in India as well as elsewhere say US, UK, Japan, Germany, France, etc. Various tiers are represented by internal audit, external audit, audit committee of the Board of Directors, statutory audit (in the case of Japan) and even strategic audit in the US. What is really surprising that despite such an elaborate control mechanism evasive practices in regard to disclosures and transparency still continue to plague the corporate world.

Any one associated with the trading MNCs in the oil sector would recall the Second World War days when, despite controls and rationing by the government and audit action of transactions by the management, artificially created scarcity of petroleum products due to collusion between sales representatives of the oil companies, dealers and the rationing authorities paralyzed the market and the users. The sales executives virtually made fortunes from the chaotic conditions like people in the medical profession in the event of an epidemic. But as the Board of Directors exercising overall control on the commercial aspects of the oil companies were located in the headquarters of the parent companies in the UK or US they did not either have details of unrecorded transactions or bother about such aberrations.

Later, even in the case of public sector undertakings where, a clear cut audit hierarchy was structured in the shape of internal audit and external audit what, really came to the notice of the public was the tip of the iceberg and the dirt never surfaced.

Virtually, the whole mass of transactions supposed to have been audited remained outside the range of visibility. Interestingly the scope of audit in such situations varied from 5–10 per cent to 100 per cent. Some transactions which were of a routine nature were subjected to a limited sample check vis-a-vis important transactions involving even 100 per cent checks. Pre-audit, concurrent audit and post-audit were imposed for further elaboration of the process.

One nefarious feature of audit in case of the public sector enterprises brought to light by the work study department was the negligence and evasive practices of internal audit departments. Detailed surveys and studies in various undertakings revealed that even educated daftries were deployed to tick the entries in the register with red ink, while the auditors were away from duty. Studies further revealed that, at times, when the auditors were assigned duties in different locations away from the office, they would rarely visit the site to do the audit yet, submit false reports to the controlling executives about completion of the job.

Thus, despite massive manpower deployed for audit work in the PSUs, hardly any useful purpose was served. However, the exceptions being when the chief executive instructed the audit department to go into complete details and check each and every transaction of an activity. At times, the vigilance department also brought to light the irregularities to the notice of the management, who in turn directed the audit section to conduct a detailed audit.

As regards external audit, the less said the better. The auditors were virtually treated like sons-in-law of the organization and given all possible facilities as demanded and desired by them. The main objective of the management being to keep the evil eye at bay and escape inconvenient questions from the auditors.

The practice is much the same in the private sector undertakings where, internal auditors proceed on the tutored lines and the external auditors coalesce for being appointed as consultants by the company on substantial fees. It is rightly said, that, one who pays the piper will call the tune. Besides, external auditors usually follow the tried and tested rule of management by exception and restrict their scope of investigations to the findings of internal audit. The executives in internal audit too have to oblige the external auditors for such cautious and friendly gestures.

Obviously, the various scams which make their appearance at high frequency in the corporate world, the banking companies, the financial institutions and the stock market corroborate the views highlighted above in ample measure. Just as they say, monsoon is a season of rains, more rains and still more rains likewise, the present financial system in the country offers opportunities for scams, more scams and still more scams. This no doubt results in deprivation of the hapless small investor of hard earned money and savings.

Recent development in the corporate world in the formation of audit committee of the board of directors is no doubt a welcome feature in the entire process of corporate governance. The Kumaramanglam Birla committee has adequately defined the composition, status, powers, role and responsibilities of the audit committee in their report. As this subject has been discussed in elaborate detail in the literature and media it may not be necessary to recount all these facts here. Yet, it may be desirable to state that audit committees success would depend on its independence and cordial relations with the various functionaries. But as the audit committee has to depend on the outside directors, they have to be careful about the role of the auditors. Incidentally, in USA the board of directors have expressed apprehensions about independence of the external auditors being compromised by their concern (auditors) for continuance of consultancy. All the same, it is necessary for the audit committee to have access to the various activities performed in the organization, with relevant expertise if considered necessary.

In the case of Japan, top tier in the audit hierarchy is represented by the Kansa-yuku, i.e. statutory auditors who monitor the entire scope of company operations and the director's activity. But here also, the interlocutors and other observators of the audit process ridicule this higher level control by the representatives of the shareholders and express apprehensions about their usefulness. They feel that, it is a mere formality without any substance.

Under the circumstances, it is necessary that the accounting profession and the corporate world as a whole stress the financial aspects of corporate governance with sincerity and commitment if the objective of transparency and full disclosure has to be achieved. Without sounding Moralistic, is I must aver that audit by one's conscience would be the ultimate weapon to prevent system abuse, murky links, unholy alliances, illicit systemic nexus amongst money traders and overall malaise in the realm of corporate governance. Also, if the auditors at all levels perform their duty with integrity more irregularities would surface in the myriad transactions undertaken by the corporates at the initial stages, and avert major scams of titanic proportions witnessed in the recent past. This way audit will reveal more than it conceals.

CHAPTER - 10

Corporate Governance : A Riddle Wrapped in Enigma

The recent corporate scams and accounting scandals have led to a flurry of activity in USA with ripple effect in the various parts of the world's advanced economies. Whether it is Japan, Germany or India, the story is the same. Virtually, all those associated with the process of governance either as a part of the sovereign authority or the various institutions like banks, auditors, chartered accountants and directors are trying to find ways and means to come out of this nefarious situation. Those not involved directly and least affected by these scams too have got worried about the state of affairs. The articles and editorials by the various intellectuals, academics and journalists are doling out sermons running into several miles of the written word. While in India it is mostly the financial dailies, which are covering these stories in elaborate detail, in other countries like the US the newspapers are flashing scam-related stories and regulatory measures either designed already or yet to be envisaged on front pages.

For instance, the Sarbane-Oxley Act 2002 signed into law by the president directing the CEOs and CFOs to certify their balance sheets under oath is expected to ameliorate the position to some extent. The other provision regarding segregation of the audit function from consultancy is also being watched with interest by the various concerned agencies. In case of India, the debate is still going on regarding the self-regulatory role of the Chartered Accountants Association of India (CAAI) despite the common argument put forth by the people that a chartered accountant or auditor who has to be paid by the client cannot afford to be objective in his approach and disposition. A debate is also raging whether SEBI should be armed with more powers to enforce the provisions of the various acts relating to corporate disclosures. The department of company affairs of the Government of India too is engaged in the exercise of effectuating stringent controls with regard to imposition of discipline in the process of corporate governance.

The various business associations, federations and chambers too are engaged in hectic activity and conducting seminars, conferences and get-togethers of the members of their bodies to evolve some suitable measures and self-regulatory mechanism in the area of a transparent and effective governance. Some of them have even started thinking seriously about recasting the role of directors of the corporate boards. Whether it is the question of compensation of the directors, the proportion of executive and non-executive directors, professional background, nature and depth of experience and the integrity of the individuals are the aspects, which are being given due consideration. The role, responsibility and liability of the directors is another area of concern for the people in power and the shareholders who are impacted directly and gravely.

The debate is continuing with regard to the effectiveness of the directors in the context of their nexus and relationship with the CEOs. Some of the whistle blowers are even raising accusing fingers on the directors for their innocuous role and acquiescence with regard to objective discharge of their ordained functions.

The recent disclosure through the report of A.F. Ferguson regarding Tata Finance Ltd. is yet another incident which has led to a controversy regarding legitimacy of the role of the consultants vis-à-vis the client. Since both the organizations, i.e. client and the consultants are held in high esteem in the country, people are finding it difficult to apportion blame squarely and exclusively on any one of them. The past history of Tata's with regard to high standards of integrity and morality maintained in their business dealings with the government, the shareholders, the customers and the common man is a potent factor which prevents people from blaming them for irregularities and under hand practices. On the other hand, Ferguson's professional standing with regard to fair dealings with their customers and uprightness in their approach are factors which speak highly of their integrity. It is virtually a situation characterized by the "holier than thou" attitude.

The top management in Tata House is, therefore, finding it difficult to absorb the blame with regard to their failure to control undesirable activities on the part of their executives and employees. While some feel that their internal auditors could be apportioned some blame for laxity and deviation from the set procedures, others feel that Ferguson's could have been slightly more meticulous in commenting on a situation about which they were not quite sure and lacked adequate data for full-scale scrutiny.

Another episode which has marred the process of the transparency in corporate governance relates to Modi Xerox. Here the bribe amounting to nearly Rs.3.5 crore given to the government agencies to obtain purchase contracts for their products goes against the principles of corporate ethics. While the modis are trying to wriggle out of the situation in all possible ways yet, the scrutiny of records of the company by the various agencies has established the fact that certain underhand deals have been scrutinized.

Whether it is a question of dictates of conscience or integrity which corporates are supposed to be guided by or, it is the rule of law which should be observed in letter and also spirit have become contentious issues.

Since no particular action has been initiated against any enterprise thus far under the provisions of corporate governance, it is difficult to say as to what extent the situation could be controlled in the country. It is also doubtful whether it would really prevent such happenings in future. In the midst of global corporate failures, it is vitally imperative that corporates make it a point to continually track public perceptions about their image and actions to escape vehement allegations. They may have to shape decisive policies to punish the guilty in this regard.

CHAPTER - 11

Corporate Governance : A Perpetual Challenge

In the last few years corporate governance has assumed great importance. This could perhaps be due to the fact, that most of the corporations now depend on the financial support of the community either, in the form of wider participation of the individual share holder or, the bulk holdings of stock by the mutual funds or various other financial institutions. The institutions could comprise of the banking companies, the pension funds and the provident fund trusts established by the Government as in the case of developed countries like the USA, Japan and Germany. This marks a radical departure from the olden days when most of the enterprises or corporations were financed by the promoters or with the borrowings arranged by the owners of the enterprises through their friends, relatives, banking companies or even private trusts. This practice was also being followed to a great extent by most of the MNCs who were running fully owned subsidiaries in various parts of the world.

The prevalent situation in the past, did not warrant much exposure on the part of corporates regarding borrowings, investment or good accounting procedures. It was assumed that, the constitution of the Board of Directors either comprising the Executive Directors, or outside directors would take the necessary precautions to ensure that the corporation was run on efficient lines. Probably, in most of the cases the vision of the CEO and the values upheld by him provided necessary guidelines and parameters for framing the mission statement, objectives and the operating philosophy. The executives who happened to have worked in senior positions in the MNCs, large private sector enterprises and family owned companies, might recall the days when the corporates hardly ever talked about governance. The public at large was mostly satisfied with the working of the MNCs, especially when they would undertake public service projects for the welfare of the community and, large business houses like Tatas, Birlas and Singhanias creating trusts for the service of the community. Besides, the consumer in general depended on the reliability of the products and the services offered by these corporations based on their corporate image. Corporate frauds regarding embezzlement of partner's money or public money were usually not heard of.

In the Indian context, the major transformation in the corporate world was brought about after the achievement of independence, and subsequently, ushering in of the era of liberalization, globalization and institutionalization. This resulted in wider participation by the public, in the various enterprises either, individually or through institutional stockholding. While the various financial institutions floated by the Government like the UTI, IDBI, ICICI, IFC and so on at the national level and similar bodies created at the state level with massive public funds in their kitty, found outlets in the shape of stockholdings of the various corporations, the individuals took recourse to buying of shares of the various companies as and when they offered their stock.

Even though the necessary regulatory steps have been taken by the authorities in this context, and suitable measures designed for checks and controls, yet a general decline in the moral standards of the public, bureaucrats, politicians and the business community has led to a major concern for effective corporate governance to ensure the safety of the various stakeholders. However, it remains a debatable issue whether the governance aspect should contribute to maximization of profits and results or, enhancing the shareholders' return and protecting the specific interest of the minority shareholders. The fact remains that, maximization of benefits for the community by improving the wealth creating capacity of the corporation would provide the defining parameters of an elaborate and viable module of corporate governance.

Certain manifestations of failure of governance, witnessed by sudden collapse of the various corporations giving sufficient proof of questionable practices, misconduct, non-existence of audit or poorly conducted audit, are the main areas of concern. In the context of corporates in India, the siphoning of public funds, unviable investments, poor planning, lack of experience and motivation for running an enterprise and other fraudulent practices have caused further anxiety to the advocates of good governance, which has assumed pervasive proportions. Even the members of the board of directors usually remain indifferent or toe the line of the chairman or the CEO to allow matters to continue. In most of the cases, the members of the board, especially the outside directors strike harmony with the CEO for their continuance and reaping the associated benefits. The inside directors are in any case docile enough to raise even a feeble voice.

It is, therefore, essential that the various business bodies like CII, FICCI, PHDCCI and various other business associations whether sector-specific or industry-specific need to institute viable research and study in the area of corporate governance. In fact, this would require an ongoing process of study to design ameliorative measures of governance, especially in India.

Perhaps, a sharper focus on the various aspects of the working of board of directors, like spelling out its work, setting specific objectives for performance and contribution, regularly appraising BODs performance against set objectives, and transparency in their activities might help the situation. Vast exposure of data, and statement of intentions displayed on full pages of economic and financial dailies and newspapers (which no one has the time and patience to read) won't help the cause of governance, unless, noble intentions match the deeds and end results expected of the corporates.

The various controlling bodies like the SEBI, BSE and DCA, the department of company affairs of the government, besides installing effective checks and controls and punitive measures to reign in the defaulters (till the present wave of malicious practices and scams continues) would need to undertake the role and responsibility of educating the corporates and public regarding the virtues of good governance. If possible examples and models of good governance be presented on a regular basis. Business of business being business, the corporate tycoons would continue to lobby (individually or through institutions) with the parliament and bureaucracy and exert influence and control on media and money providers-banks, financial bodies and others- sometimes, with undesirable consequences.

CHAPTER - 12

Corporate Mergers : Human Resource Implications

The process of globalization and integration of the world economy has led to a spate of mergers, acquisitions and takeovers. This perhaps has been occasioned due to the fear of competition and the anxiety on the part of corporates either to devour weak players or to confront head on large giants who are out manoeuvring existing conglomerates. Another aspect which has ushered in the process of strategic alliances is the vaulting ambition of the corporates to outsize the various rivals. It seems that there is a battle for size, space, dominance and visibility. Earlier mergers in the corporate world were perpetrated mostly due to progressive nationalization of the various industrial enterprises. For instance, formation of Coal India and Hindustan Steel as also SAIL subsequently had led to the acquisition process of small enterprises in the private sector. The various entities of Coal India like the Eastern Coal Fields, Western Coal Fields and Central Coal Fields, etc. had also absorbed a very large number of private coal mines soon after nationalization. Similarly, Hindustan Steel Ltd. had grabbed a number of iron ore mines, coal mines and dolomite mines. The underlying pattern has been manifest in this phenomenon :

i) Public sector enterprises acquiring/merging small private units.

ii) Large private sector enterprises like TISCO taking over smaller private enterprises.

iii) Multinational companies entering into strategic alliances or outright acquisition of the various units in their respective field or activity.

Human Resource Profile

The above situation has impacted the HR profile in many ways on different occasions. As an instance, the various coal mines which were taken over by Coal India had a diverse set of human resource policies and manpower profile as under :

i) The private mines were mostly owned by foreign companies.

ii) Some of the units were also run by Indian entrepreneurs.

iii) Top level executives in the private sector, especially the top two or three positions were held by the expatriates.

iv) The middle and lower level executives were usually Indian except for a few technical experts.

v) The non-executive staff, especially in highly skilled categories too comprised some foreigners.

vi) The skilled and unskilled workers were mostly Indian.

vii) The style of management of the expatriates was mainly autocratic, indifferent and impersonal. While they maintained the grand Mughal style of living, the labour class mostly lived in small huts or housing clusters almost resembling slums and ghettos. Employees were thus treated as a commodity.

viii) The pay package of the top level executives could be as much as 100 times of the unskilled or even skilled Indian labour.

ix) In the case of junior and middle executives as also workers (mostly nationals) the hierarchy was quite tall and artificial levels were interposed without entailing requisite responsibility and authority. Even in the case of workers the number of levels could be as many as 15 to 20 giving them a feeling of elation while being moved from one level to another. In some cases job clusters were formed consisting of 3 to 4 levels to ensure that an employee remained in the same position for a longer duration with marginal increase in emoluments from grade to grade. Even in the case of junior and middle level executives recourse was taken to the cluster system.

x) While for workers promotions were based on seniority, in the case of executives' escalation was usually oriented to so-called merit or favourtism.

xi) For executives disparate pay packages were evolved and no uniform approach was followed. At the same level and for the same responsibility, the executives could have vast disparities in perks and privileges.

xii) Welfare measures and other benefits for the workers were mostly governed and dictated by the legal provisions.

Implications

i) As against the practices in the private sector, the public sector or even large private enterprises like Tatas had a well structured hierarchy for workers, executives and the top brass.

ii) Intake points for the unskilled, skilled, highly skilled and the executive categories were well defined in terms of education and experience. Entry level basic pay and scales too were designed specifically.

iii) The number of positions was decided on the basis

of Industrial Engineering studies with some marginal adjustment here and there.

iv) In the case of workers, promotions were oriented to seniority. Executives earned their spurs by seniority-cum-merit or merit-cum-seniority.

v) Generally promotion policies were well defined in terms of eligibility in the form of education, experience and number of years put in, in a particular scale.

vi) The system of recruitment, placement and advancement was quite transparent and the line of promotion or the career path for non-executives and executives was well chartered.

vii) Labour unions participated actively in the formation of personnel policies and procedures for recruitment, placement, training and promotion of workers. The labour as well as executive manpower was reviewed and assessed from time to time keeping in view the business plan of the organization.

viii) In many enterprises specific manpower cells were constituted to undertake exercise in manpower planning and development.

ix) In large private sector enterprises like the Tatas and Birlas a somewhat similar approach was followed.

x) The employees in the small private sector were mostly in higher age groups in the worker and executive categories, which were in existence prior to merger in the large private sector undertakings or public sector enterprises.

xi) The level of education of the workers as well as executives was of a lower order in the unorganized enterprises.

xii) The workers were mostly on the roll of sub contractors or contractors; while only a few hands were on the regular roll of the company.

Assimilation Exercise

On merger or takeover the managements were faced with a serious problem of assimilation of the workers and executives from the smaller enterprises into a big corporation. Some of the following measures were designed by Coal India, SAIL and Tatas to tackle the problem of manpower rationalization:

i) At the worker level, specific intake points and lines of promotion were defined for different educational levels and job requirements.

ii) A trade off was struck for experience and education in the case of senior workers of private enterprises.

iii) Some employees were placed in higher pay scales while others were provided personal grades till they got absorbed in the regular categories and pay scales.

iv) In some cases even personal job titles had to be retained for such workers.

v) To the junior and middle level workers options were given to accept a particular pay scale or improve their academic qualifications to match the well educated executive categories of the large undertakings.

vi) For others long experience with lower education was equated with higher qualifications and less experience prescribed for an executive position.

vii) Special training programmes were organized for the development of workers and executives.

viii) Detailed manpower studies were undertaken to assess requirements in terms of levels, skills, age and experience required for a particular job.

ix) Redundant manpower generated in the process was either re-deployed with suitable training or given compensation for voluntary separation.

x) In the case of senior executives, screening was done through exhaustive interviews for placement in suitable slots.

xi) Some of the executives were retained in their existing jobs by virtue of proficiency attained by them.

Present Scenario

In addition to mergers, takeovers, acquisitions and strategic alliance a lot of restructuring and divestment is taking place in the corporate world both in private and public sector enterprises as also multinationals. Particularly, in the case of MNCs and large private sector enterprises the myriad problems encountered on the manpower front are as under :

i) Job titles, authority structure, responsibility levels and operational freedom are affected by mergers. Normally, the acquiring companies dictate and dominate merged enterprise.

ii) A large number of executives opt out of the job in the merged companies. The workers keep fighting a losing battle for protecting their interests.

iii) Various problems like relocation, disruption in

family life, changed job profile and absorption confront the executives.

iv) Some of the units and divisions are closing down permanently.

v) The process of mergers and takeovers is thus taking a heavy toll of executives' emotional and motivational disposition.

In view of the above, it would be helpful if specific efforts are made to survey the manpower position as also study human resource policies of the varying merging units to arrive at appropriate human resource strategy for assimilating the manpower into the main stream without much pain and privation. Redundancies, if any, could be removed with adequate compensation or redeployed with requisite training in different jobs. Guidelines could be sought from the past practices outlined in the foregoing paras. This way endemic brutal restructuring caused by de-mergers, mergers and mega-mergers with deleterious impact on the morale and well-being of the human resources would be minimized.

CHAPTER - 13

Corporate Change with Less Pain and Strain

Of late, the subject of change has come under sharp focus. Change is usually of two types :

i) evolutionary or first order change, and

ii) revolutionary or second order change.

The change process is portrayed by the change force in terms of weak, moderate and strong. The corporates endeavouring to cope with the change process assume pro-active, reactive and radical stances depending on the change force in the above order and the level of resistance rising from low to high.

Corresponding to the change force intensity and the fact whether the organization is open to change, can be opened to change or closed to change, the path of change is characterized as continuous, mixed or discontinuous. Obviously pro-active leadership remains alert and keeps its antenna attuned to capture the straws in the wind and reflect the environmental scenario on the corporate radar screen. The reactive leadership endeavours to adapt itself and the organization by realigning the organization structure and taking recourse to patching in its systems, processes and people related policies and interventions. The radical leadership could bludgeon the organizational system with re-engineering, ruthless downsizing and drastic cost reduction measures.

Vital Components

The three vital elements of an organization, namely,

systems, processes and people which bear the impact of any type of change force need to be kept under constant vigil to obviate the undesirable impact on the optimum performance of the entity. Consequently, the intervention strategy of an organization to cope with or manage change could focus on individuals and their roles, groups and their structure, processes and their life span and the enterprise as a whole in terms of strategy, systems, operating paradigms and mindset.

Experience tells, that there is no arrival point for change as the direction and destination are indeterminate. Besides, change could affect people and organizations in different ways depending on their capabilities to maintain equilibrium between the driving and resisting forces.

The factors which usually impact an organization could be enumerated as under :

1. Technology
2. Employees
3. Social trends
4. Suppliers
5. Economy
6. Markets and customers

Context

However, there is no specific sequence or fixed quantum of change force exerted by these factors. Hence one could assume that the context rather than content and size of these elements would be the focal area of analysis, study and treatment. As such an organization could select any of these factors at a given juncture to change the order of change. For instance, in the case of employees, one could discern as to where the change hurts, i.e.

head, heart or guts. Also it would be desirable to comprehend as to why resistance stems from the employees.

The following aspects would need to be examined to understand the situation :

1. Threat to status, self-esteem, power base, control of destiny and loss of perceived benefits.

2. Uncongenial organizational climate in respect of 'OCTAPACE' values, i.e. openness, confrontation, trust, authenticity, pro-action, autonomy, collaboration and experimentation.

   Note: When these values operate below the desirable level, organization is normally not amenable to change initiatives.

3. Fear of the unknown, failure, looking stupid, exposed and vulnerable.

4. High level of anxiety and stress due to threat to the established skills, team relationships, customs and conventions and operating regimes and practices.

5. Unwillingness to part with the entrenched mindset and the reluctance to let go.

   It would also be instructive to gauge the impact and the typical response an individual demonstrates to a significant change which could manifest in the following order :-

   1. Shock
   2. Defensive retreat
   3. Acknowledgement and acceptance
   4. Adaptation

Particularly, the intensity of shock could be quite cataclysmic, painful, demoralizing and destab; lizing. It could badly puncture the ego and destroy the self-image of an individual irreparably.

Cases

A few case histories would help to illustrate the situation described in the foregoing paras.

Note : Names of the individuals have been changed to obviate disclosure of identity.

1. Ramdev Mehta was an ardent aspirant for the post of MD in a public sector undertaking. He kept a close watch on senior level moves in the organization. In the year 1991 the CEOs slot became available as the incumbent decided to opt out of the job and grab some top level position in a private undertaking on a lucrative pay packet.

   Mehta being dead set to avail himself of the God-sent opportunity mounted a powerful all pervasive lobby in bureaucratic, political and other power centres to sieze the position. He almost took it for granted, when a communication form informal channels reinforced his self-perception to be the legitimate successor to the top spot. The news spread like a wild fire and the elbow guys got engaged in organizing a general ceremonial function to incarnate the corporate king. As the corporate world, especially the PSUs (where one earns spurs mostly by flattery in the so-called merit oriented system) excel in the art of flattery, a large crowd of sycophants and their spouses converged on the scene. Just as the coronation ceremony was about to conclude a message was flashed from the ministry announcing the appointment of Rattan Kapila as the Managing Director. This sent shock waves amongst the revellers and the entire ceremony came a cropper. Mehta almost fainted with shock and had to be rushed to the ICU of the company hospital. However, timely and intensive efforts on the part of doctors saved Mehta's life. Later with the help of counselling from the Chairman and other members of the Board he was made to recover from the shock.

2. In yet another case, in 1996-97 due to sudden down turn in the steel market, in process inventory and the stock of finished items got piled up in the factories of a company. Despite, various measures like cut back in production, cost cutting, price reduction, liberal credit provision and persuasion with the customers to lift stocks, cash flow position did not improve. At the same time suppliers, vendors and financial institutions kept up pressure to recover their dues from the proprietors. Consequently, the position became grave and management got into a serious dilemma.

   However, when all efforts failed to a bring about recovery, management decided to take drastic action in the shape of 'lockout' in the various factories. This action caused provocation to the workers and union leaders and resulted initially in a slow down and work to rule. Later, on losing patience the workers reacted violently in some cases and went on strike in one of the factories. The management seized this opportunity to declare a lockout. In sympathy, workers in other factories followed suit.

   This led to all sorts of unpleasant things and legal and illegal actions on both sides. Some workers left in desperation and others parted after availing themselves of some monetary compensation. In due course, all the fac tories were closed down and the firm went out of the steel business.

Perhaps, timely action to educate the workers and supervisors about the gravity market situation and the need to take some remedial steps and offer of separation benefits would have avoided bloodshed and other unseemly actions on both sides.

3. VRS in banks in recent months provides ample testimony to the fact that a good will gesture and use of discretion by the employees has made the task of restructuring, downsizing and mechanizing the various operations smooth, painless and enduring. Also a radical and revolutionary change order has been initiated in a harmonious, amicable and acceptable way especially when PSU banks were on the ropes in the face of brutal competition from private sector banks and nothing short of drastic retrenchment action would have created paralyzing fear amongst employees. No doubt during the transition phase both customers and bankers have to face some hardship owing to temporary disruption.

Pacing

These case histories bring to light the need to manage change, especially by pacing it with the people in the organization who are affected gravely. In a situation like this, person focused OD interventions come in handy as stated below :

1) The leadership has to educate the employees about the limited capability of an organization to match the unlimited aspirations of an individual. Perhaps, a trade off would need to be struck to plug the divergent gap.

2) Coaching and mentoring the employees at all levels including the CEO would need to be taken recourse to.

3) Employees need to be energized, empowered and engaged in the change process. An ongoing OD process will have to be set in motion to activate the employees

to commit and involve themselves in the self-learning process and develop a high level of tolerance to confront the unsavoury situation and absorb the pain as and when threatened and unnerved by some sudden discontinuities and deviations from the chartered pace or path. This would enable them to cope with the change process and even change the order of change.

CHAPTER - 14

Changing the Corporate Change Order

As highlighted in the previous chapter the various factors which usually impact organization are employees technology, social trends, suppliers, economy, markets and customers. As the employee factor has already been discussed, the present write up confines the discussion to the impact of technology on change. So as to be able to comprehend, as to what influence the technology can exert on the organization, its structure, processes, people and institutions, it would be relevant to examine the following aspects :

1. Nature, scope and depth of technology, the purpose to be achieved and the likely benefits to accrue to the organization in terms of productivity growth and competitiveness.

2. The extent to which the existing machines, equipment and the processes including regimes would need to be changed.

3. The financial implications of the new technology.

4. The extent of planning, designing, implementing and maintaining the new systems required vis-à-vis the existing situation.

5. Adequacy of the present infrastructure and the need to develop new infrastructural facilities.

6. The vision and the strategy relevant for the organizational renewal, growth and survival in the context of changed technology and its impact on the stakeholders.

In any change effort, the focus being on the human factor it would be imperative to examine the OD characteristics in terms of organizational system and its components, interaction and interrelation amongst the various sub systems, use of relevant agency, internal/external as change agents, problem-solving approach, learning by experience and the usual OD methdology in terms of diagnosis, feedback, implementation, monitoring, evaluating and repeating the cycle if required.

This being so, OD values and the basic assumption about humans, i.e. good and self-disciplined vs bad and undisciplined, difference about their background, experience, information, ideas, view point and personality as also need of the people to express feelings and emotions and to seek confirmation and support for their behaviour, will need to be taken into reckoning.

Other related issues as reflected in the organizational climate, namely 'Octapace Values' (Openness, Confrontation, Trust, Authenticity, Pro-action, Autonomy, Collaboration and Experimentation) would also need to be examined for putting equal emphasis on task (in terms of technology, systems, procedures and techniques) and people to ensure that the managerial grid which is often used as an instrument of OD for diagnosing the organization and finding its suitability for not only managing the change process but also altering it if necessary.

Sweeping Technological Change

In the modern times, the most sweeping technological change which has manifested itself in the Indian economy or even the world economy, is information technology and its associated hardware and software dimensions. In the Indian context, the process of change management of the IT revolution could be illustrated by the various steps initiated by the Government of Andhra Pradesh in the recent past.

To start with, the government has crafted its vision and strategy about the future in the context of information technology.

It has also intiated specific measures to communicate the change vision to the masses. Some of the salient steps taken by the Government of Andhra Pradesh are enumerated in this context as under :-

i) Ushering in the process of e-governance by involvement of the people of the State in the process of change.

ii) Selection of bureaucrats from the various government departments for exposing them to intensive training in the area of information technology and management of knowledge who in turn would train, coach and mentor other employees in different departments of the Government.

iii) Broad banding of digital connectivity with a view to ensure IT has a pervasive impact on the working of the people. This shows that determined efforts would need to be made to manage and alter the governing process with the use of IT.

Banking World

Of late, a number of measures have been initiated in the banking world to make use of the information technology for rendering fast service to the clients in respect of their products and other offerings. For instance, the measures designed by the HDFC Bank in the shape of ATMs, phone banking, net banking, mobile banking and international debit card are the devices to assist mobile clients for conducting their business transactions instantly any time, anywhere in the world. The customers could address enquiries regarding their balance, payment of utility bills, stop payment of issues, viewing of last three transactions as also details of fixed deposits on the mobile. Considering these developments, it would be necessary that the relevant OD interventions are invoked in their concerned organizations, with a view to ensure proper interfacing between the people and technology. In case, suitable OD measures are not initiated, not only would adoption of new technology be delayed, but it would also create maladjustment and affect timely execution of the job.

The following case would illustrate the point that when adequate measures are not designed to manage technology, what adverse effect it could have on the morale and motivation of the employees as also delay the pace of technological change.

Case

In the early 1960s, a multinational decided to go in for computerization of the sales and marketing activity with particular focus on the generation of data relating to daily, weekly and monthly sales of its various products in different branches and divisions of the company. The intention being to centralize the acquision of data at the headquarters of the company at Mumbai (then Bombay) on the basis of reports generated on the computer by the various Divisions and the Branches. While their objective was quite laudable and tenable and in sync with the times yet, the whole approach misfired in the initial stages as no opportunity was provided to the executives and the staff to get acquainted with the concepts, application capability and the operating features of computer-based systems. Besides, no specific training was provided to the employees in the branches and the divisions before undertaking the process of computerization. A brief communication from the Head Office along with the operating manual designed by the IBM were the only material passed on to the branches for implementation of the new system. As the executives were not preparedfor the change and were also not willing to take pains involved in learning the system, they passed on the responsibility to the non-executive employees, namely supervisors and the head clerks to get the new system implemented on their own.

The employees were issued instructions to study the manuals and learn the working of the computers on their own initiative and institute the new system by a specific deadline. As the appropriate steps were not taken in time, the learning process on the part of the employees proved quite arduous and painful. However, being threatened by the loss of employment they had to adopt the new system at the cost of considerable strain and loss of time. This way, the usual phenomenon which often manifests itself in the case of significant changes in an organization led to the following consequences for the employees in traversing the change path :-

1. Shock

2. Defensive retreat

3. Acknowledgement and acceptance

4. Adaptation

In the foregoing context, it is imperative that the corporate management initiate the requisite OD measures before the adoption of any new techniques and technology. This would enable the management to manage the change as also alter the change order.

CHAPTER – 15

Emerging Corporate - Philosophy "Yeh Dil Mange More"

Pepsi's punch line "Yeh Dil Maange More" seems to be the result of an in-depth and enduring research in the realms of human behaviour. Though the context is Pepsi-specific, yet the message is universal. The corporate world has yet to discover a more crisp, cutting and concise line or a slogan which would represent the materialistic or spiritual outlook and disposition of mankind. In fact even spirituals, intellectuals, clergy and all powerful monarchs fall prey to such human frailties, though for different reasons. However, in this article observations are restricted to the business world.

Corporates are caught up in a cobweb of conflicting and opposing forces. Pulls and pressures from the various stakeholders make the situation all the more complex and vexed. A brief description of the motives of the vested interests would present a lucid exposition of this phenomenon. While corporate history is replete with incidents and happenings which have been plaguing them at different junctures during booms and busts it may be instructive to confine the scope of discussion to the present state of affairs.

For the sake of clarity and focus, it would be appropriate to take up the case of the myriad stakeholders one by one as described below :

Promoters and Entrepreneurs

The basic desire of an entrepreneur is to ensure fast growth and sustainability of his enterprise. According to his conviction, instincts and experience he elucidates certain principles and evolves values and vision to attain his mission. The level of aspiration is subject to change depending upon the resource availability, competitive scenario and the strengths and weaknesses of the enterprise at any given point of time. All the same, the promoter would expect his business to grow on a geometrical scale and the turnover and profits to accelerate at high velocity.

He endeavours to take on the competition and leap frog to number one position in double quick time. With every success his ambition flares and he looks forward to dominating the corporate scene. He crafts strategies to expand his market, product line, brands and customer base. The sky is thus the limit to growth and expansion, organic or through mergers and takeovers. Higher and still higher market cap boosting bottom line, wider market space and glittering corporate image constitute other manifestations of desire. Recognition as the best promoter, caring employer, progressive entrepreneur and transformational leader assume high significance in his scale of concern. Thus the more he achieves, the more he aspires to achieve. His bundle of wants too gets magnified. This way PEPSI's ad punch line "Yeh Dil Maange More" would be an apt description of his disposition.

Shareholders

Shareholders expect the share price of holdings to sky rocket in the least possible time. Even when the market is passing through a bearish phase these people would like to visualize a bullish trend in their stocks. Any quantum of hike in the share value would always be welcome. Besides, they always endeavour to expand their shareholdings in volumetric terms. This urge seems perennial and they want more and more.

Trade Unions

After establishing a firm base in a particular enterprise, unions always look forward to expanding their horizons. While, within the enterprise union leaders seek a wider power base through enlarged membership and access to the management, outside they attempt a bigger role in the industry and ultimately at the national level or even international level. There is an inner urge on the part of leaders to develop platform skills and staying power to accomplish their objectives, come into the visible range and acquire celebrity status and perhaps even the position of political bigwigs. The desire to grab more and more underpins the union leaders' strategy, tactics and modus operandi in the area of their activity. Every union leader tries to outwit others to hog the limelight and win members' favour by wrenching as many benefits as possible for them, from the management or proprietors. The charter of demands keeps lengthening menacingly and never gets restrained.

Employees

Frequent and fast promotions, perks, monetary and non-monetary benefits, incentives, statutory bonus, productivity bonus, profit sharing in some form or the other comprise the wish list of employees. If one employee gets promoted after a gap of three years from one step to the next in the hierarchy, the other expects to grab this opportunity after two years. As such employees' satisfaction looks like a receding mirage. This poses a constant challenge to the management to invent new means and modes of motivation to keep employees' morale soaring. Thus it becomes a tug of war between an enterprise's limited ability to cater to employees' never ending demands and cravings.

Executives

Executives at all levels–junior, middle, senior and top, are usually fired with the ambition to achieve more and more in terms of rank in the hierarchy, status, power, influence and recognition. Corporates often exploit this weakness of the executives by setting stretch goals, moving and escalating targets, expanded span of activity, increased volume of work, responsibility and accountability.

In an effort to measure up to corporate expectations executives often lose work-life balance and end up as workaholics. At times, this could cause stress and burnout for some of them. However, despite such hazards and consequences, the perennial process of endeavouring to accomplish one's desires and legitimate or illogical wants against various odds, hurdles and pitfalls continues.

Likewise suppliers, vendors, dealers and customers keep pressing their demands and enterprise on a regular basis. The process keeps evolving in the cycle of demands and wants keep manifesting themselves on an eternal basis.

CHAPTER – 16

Corporate Job-Hopping

Job change is a by-product of industrial civilization. The faster the pace of industrial revolution, the more frequent becomes the process of job hopping. Industrially advanced societies are witnessing this phenomenon on a much larger scale than the comparatively less advanced economies. While some consider job-hopping a fad, others deem it as a necessary evil. Some even consider it as a vital imperative for the growth of the industry and the individual simultaneously. A higher level of educational preparation, vocational exposure and professional growth accelerate the incidence of job-hopping.

The arousal of ambition amongst the individuals, for assumed or, real growth prospects elsewhere spurs them to look for greener pastures and wider vistas in other organizations. Social prestige attached to the element of growth, and achievement in terms of hierarchical position, give further impetus to the individual for changing jobs. Working conditions within the industry, the culture, the climate, the value system and the individual's capacity to adjust within these environments determine his choice for a changeover. Placement in a particular function, job aptitude, the desire to enjoy freedom, independence, delegation of powers, scope for interaction with peers on a lateral basis and individuals at higher levels in other departments, as also the management policies prescribed for reward and punishment instil a desire in the mind of an individual for changing the place of work.

The past rate of growth of the individual in the organization, prospects for the future compared to his colleagues as also the various people in the organization as a whole, often prompt the individual to opt for a change. The pay packet, stock option plan, bonus system, profit sharing in the present organization as against the prospective employer, reinforce the decision of the individual to look for better prospects. The pace of growth of an individual in his organization vis-à-vis his friends and relatives in different organizations also impel him to take recourse to job–hopping for equally alluring and rapid prospects for growth.

Modes

The change of job could materialize in one of the following ways :

1. From one organization to another organization, dealing either with the same product or a different product.

2. From one organization operating within the country to another organization operating on a multinational scale.

Frequency

The incidence of job-hopping varies not only in respect of the individuals but also in terms of occupations, professions, functions and organizations. Moreover, the practices of job-hopping vary from country to country. While in some countries like Japan, the incidence of job hopping is quite low on account of a long–standing tradition of lifelong loyalty to the organization, in other countries in Europe and America the frequency of job hopping is rather high. Furthermore, the incidence of job–hopping varies from sector to sector. For instance, while the incidence of job-hopping is lower in the public sector in India, it is higher in the private sector. The frequency of job-hopping also depends on the pace of growth of a particular individual in the past and the scope of advancement in future. For instance, the fast rate of growth of Electronic Data Processing in countries like India offers much better prospects for growth to the individuals as compared to other functions like Materials, Production and Personnel. Whereas, in some functions the rate of turnover (due to job–hopping) has been of the order of 10 per cent or so in certain organizations, in other cases it could have been as high as 30 to 40 per cent. The frequency of job-hopping also varies with the phase of career. Normally the tendency to change a job is much stronger in the earlier phase of one's career than at a later stage, say around the mid–30s. Moreover the rate of job–shopping slows down as one progresses in career from the mid-30s to the mid-40s. Virtually from the mid-40s onwards, the rate of change of job becomes negligible. The frequency of job-changing is also said to be higher, in the case of people, with higher educational and professional qualifications than their peers and colleagues with lower academic achievement.

IT Scenario

Job hopping has assumed the proportions of plague. Virtually there is the killer urge to change jobs frequently and rapidly in the initial career phases. Greenhorns are especially prone to the allure of greener pastures elsewhere. Impulsive forces keep prompting the young brigade to look for more lucrative opportunities for instant gratification and esteem in IT circles. Even executives perched at the appex are not immune to the magic of Eldorado. Quitting an organization does not create qualms or convulsions. Self-serving motives and climb to the executive hierarchy at an accelerated pace in double quick time has substituted concern for loyalty and longevity. As frequent moves necessitate a new work environment, different sets of people, diverse locations, dissimilar class of stakeholders (like vendors, customers, stockholders, peers and others) the need to enhance emotional maturity, equilibrium and change in mindset has accelerated the process of knowledge acquisition, skill development and grasp for IT-related issues.

A virtual move from a set of familiar environs to the land of assumed promise and prosperity in an unfamiliar and uncertain situation results in a sort of blind man's buff for the various aspirants. Exiting from the so-called old industries and establishing nexus with the new economy has given rise to a sort of exodus at all levels. Allure of enabling measures which propel an individual to stake his career are the venture capital providers, incubator services and Internet facility. In this rush for assumed wealth acquisition some of the fundamental aspects for seeking new job opportunities are being given short shrift. Some of the common features discernible in this move could be enumerated as under :

1. Aspirants are vague about the nature, type and potential of the new venture.

2. The skill set required to grasp the new job.

3. Inadequate knowledge of the market, the product and the type of service which could be offered to the clients.

4. The structure of the job and the organization, the product and the service needed by the customer.

5. The nature and type of customer and the pattern of demand.

6. The volume of financial resources in the shape of seed capital and working capital and working capital required.

7. Poor knowledge of mainstream activity, the selling prospects and the cash flow prospects in the new venture.

8. The rules of the game and the tricks of the trade required to deal with the new people and problems.

9. The nature, type and level of infrastructure required for conducting the activity.

10. Lack of detailed knowledge of the processes involved in the new business activity.

Loss vs Gain

Job-hopping is not entirely an undesirable feature of organizational life. It has both merits and demerits. To that extent it is not an unmixed blessing. May be advantages of job-hopping outweigh its disadvantages in certain situations and vice-versa. Also at times, job-hopping may bestow positive benefits on an individual and at other times it may prove totally infructuous.

Some of the apparent gains and losses of job-hopping could be outlined as under:

Merits

1. Job-hopping impels one to take recourse to learning on a continuing basis. Hence the learning curve maintains a steady upturn.

2. It keeps the individual agile mentally and improves his physical mobility.

3. Job-hopping enables the individual to adapt and adjust to diverse environments more easily than non-job hoppers.

4. Job-changing may result in higher pace of growth, job satisfaction and achievement of one's career goals.

5. Job-hopping inculcates in the individual a spirit of competition and challenge to acquire new and better jobs.

6. Exposure to different jobs helps to enrich experience, knowledge and builds up capacity and potential to handle bigger and better jobs with confidence and courage.

7. Change of jobbrings about a state of equilibrium, in terms of rate and frequency of job-hopping in different organizations, which are exposed either to a very low

rate of job–hopping or to a very high rate of employee departures.

8. Job-hopping helps to promote the pace of growth of the industry as experience gained by the individuals in different organizations contributes to the overall well-being of the society.

Demerits

1. Job-hopping leads to unstable conditions in an organization.

2. It makes an individual restless, impulsive and rash at times.

3. Job-hopping brings down the element of loyalty of an individual to the organization.

4. Job-hoppers become callous and indifferent to the interest of their colleagues and the organization for which they work.

5. The proverb " a rolling stone gathers no mass" is more true of job-hoppers than anybody else.

6. Job-hopping does not allow an individual to gain sufficient experience of a particular job and to contribute to the overall improvement in the job situation.

7. The job-hopper may be characterized as an unreliable and shallow individual.

8. The individuals changing jobs frequently may not be entrusted with responsible jobs in the organization till their credentials or loyalty is proved to the organization.

9. Job-hopping may not necessarily satisfy the hidden or explicit urges of individuals for better prospects in terms of reward, job satisfaction, independence, self-actualization and achievement of targetted goals. Each organization would need to reckon the impact of job hopping on its working efficiency and tailor its approach either, to encourage the individuals to opt for change or, remain stayput. May be, the culture of job changing proves to be a boon, especially when redundancies occur and individuals exposed to the process of job-hopping accept changed situation reality and seek reemployment voluntarily. Perhaps, in other situations an organization may have to be stripped off of certain undesirable elements, who do not fit well into the company milieu.

Also the various organizations may have to design specific measures to obviate the sudden impact of hopping on its manpower structure with undesirable distortions. In any case, job-hopping has become an irrevocable fact of life and both the individuals and the organization would have to bear with it.

CHAPTER - 17

Corporate Hierarchy : A Vexed Dilemma

Life in a business enterprise has never been an unmixed blessing. When the hierarchy in the structure is tall, the numerous steps involved in the upward journey extend the gap between the initial rung and the appex intractably. And when the tiers are compressed, the time span to traverse each level increases inexorably. While a tall hierarchy dilutes the quantum of responsibility, power, autonomy, span and access to resources, the sandwiched structure provides disproportionate exposure vis-à-vis the quantum of experience, maturity and emotional stability required to match the challenge of the job. A bloated middle in the hierarchy creates a bulge and narrows the base with too many executives to supervise the job of too few hands. And a flattened top in the structure creates an inverted pyramid with divided and diffused responsibility, distorted job content, overlap in activities and a wrangling brigade. Objectives and key result areas (KRAs) of each position become warped and indistinct. The same people who vigorously pursue their career prospects and lobby for a spur, do not relish the pursuit of their peers for a similar mission. Oddly enough, though, the sheen and the glamour perceived in the next layer vanishes soon after the phoney title san substance has been attained. In fact, soon one gets disillusioned and blames management policies for such an eventuality.

However, to resolve the issue, it is imperative that a clear understanding is created in the minds of the individuals to appreciate the need for finding a balance between their unlimited aspiration and the limited ability of an organization to cater to their cravings. Also, there is need to conceptualize an hierarchical module which unequivocally delineates a promotional hierarchy from operating levels and decision-making levels. These levels could be visualized and portrayed as under :

Promotional Levels - An Illustration

Director		
ED		
Sr.	V.P.	Asstt. DGM
	VP	Sr. Mgr.
Sr.	GM	Mgr
	GM	Dy. Mgr I
Addl.	GM	Dy. Mgr II
Jt.	GM	Asstt. Mgr
Sr.	DGM	Jr. Mgr — etc.
	DGM	

Operating hierarchy, on the other hand, could be compressed into 4/5 levels depending on the volume, variety, span and dispersion of activity and the decision load depending on the capability of individual decision takers. A specimen of such an hierarchy could be charted as below :-

Operating Levels - An Illustration

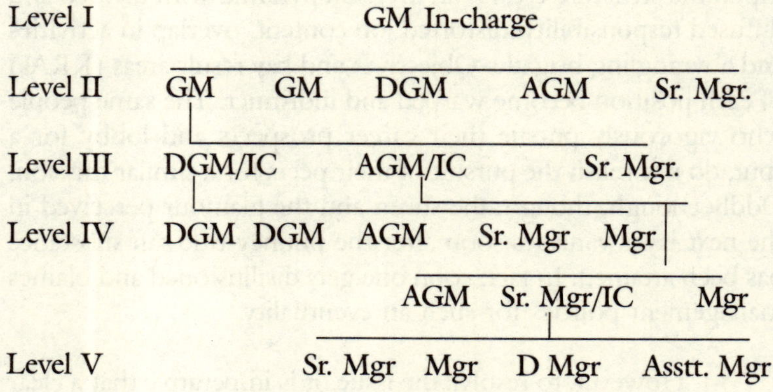

These levels could be reduced further depending upon the various variables like volume of activity, span of control and size of the territory of operation.

On the other hand, decision levels could be located either

one step above the point of coordination or cross-over or even two steps upwards depending on the corporate philosophy regarding delegation of power, empowerment, ability of the executives adorning the myriad coordinating positions and so on. However, it is essential that an adequate communication process is established for continuous education of the executives in this regard and they are made to understand and appreciate the organizational imperatives vis-à-vis their aspirations for advancement in the hierarchy with commensurate rewards, perks and perceived status. May be, the extant structure evolved over a span of time does not offer simultaneous opportunity for promotion to the next higher rank and assumed and established benefits for coordinating or decision taking levels in the corporate hierarchy. While in the public sector usually seniority still rules the roost, in most of the private undertakings local or multinational merit holds sway for the controlling positions.

Fortunately, in the IT world the knowledge worker is rather oblivious of the rank concept and looks forward to an opportunity for learning, job satisfaction, a fat pay packet and empowerment to design his job and guide his destiny.

A few examples from the corporate world would illustrate the proposition in a clear and comprehensible manner.

In most of the public and private sector enterprises indulgent policies regarding inflated hierarchy, alluring job titles, diluted responsibility and overwhelming routine and repetitive components in the job content are manifestations of this scenario. As already stated in the foregoing paras, constant endeavour on the part of the corporates to keep their executives motivated and align their policies with the latter's aspirations to wean them away from outside distractions of weightier job titles and still more lucrative pay packets creates a compulsive situation for designing such psychological barriers. For instance, in SAIL plants most of the production shops and services and maintenance departments which were manned by engineers of the rank of Superintendent are now being managed by Chief Superintendents, AGMs,

DGMs, GMs or even Executive Directors. The title of an individual depends on his length of service and stay in a particular rank irrespective of the responsibility level.

This way the number of GMs, DGMs, AGMs and Superintendents has increased manifold.

ONGC, Coal India and many other undertakings present a similar scenario. In fact, in some of these enterprises the number of GMs is much greater now than entry level executives strength a few years ago.

In the private sector too, even small enterprises have been forced to design myriad titles like Sr. President, President, Vice President, Jr. President and so on.

Bureaucracy too has not lagged behind in this regard as job titles like Chief Secretary, Secretary, Additional Secretary, Joint Secretary, Deputy Secretary and Under Secretary have been invented to cater for the cravings of their officers.

Under the circumstances, recourse to the concept of operational and promotional hierarchy assumes relevance and legitimacy till the corporate world has fully adjusted to the realities of a flat and lean structure in the executive hierarchy which, perhaps, could be visualized as the future organizational paradigm. In the meantime, both the hierarchies, i.e. tall and short will need to be kept operative.

CHAPTER - 18

Corporate Succession:A Vital Imperative

Business enterprises usually outlive the promoters unless marred by some upheaval or extinction. This happens when they are unable to cope with the pace, intensity and direction of change. It is therefore essential that all such enterprises which survive the ravages of time or grow in size, shape or territorial dimensions continue to have an uninterrupted chain of executive and entrepreneurial hierarchy. Particularly, at this juncture of corporate history, succession has assumed a great relevance. This is primarily due to the emergence of the process of urbanization and spread of education when, a large segment of the populace has to take recourse to paid employment in the business entities for their active working life.

In early days, family members were the natural choice as the business assets mostly belonged to the family and risks or gains mainly affected their lives and prospects. Also, due to limited size of business and little scope for mobility of the siblings, the reigns of business remained in the hands of members of the family. Hence, not much attention was paid to the aspect of succession.

However, all those, who have observed the changing skyline of the business world since the early 1950s would have marked myriad changes in the scope, structure, diversity and overall dimensions of an industrial enterprise.

One major factor, which has lent urgency to the concept and process of succession planning has been the institutionalization of the factors of production-land, labour, capital and (of late) knowledge.

As it is, different sectors of the economy go in for the

succession process in different ways as described in the following paras :

Government Enterprises – Soon after the country gained independence, a number of enterprises emerged on the national scene modelled the national policies and economic planning. Initially, mostly, government employees from the administrative service-State or Centre-were deployed in these units in senior and top level positions. While some changes have been made for the deployment of executives in the central PSUs, in the case of state-level enterprises most of the positions at the apex of the hierarchy are adorned by government officials. Almost all the SEs in Punjab, Haryana, Himachal, UP and other states are occupied by administrative cadres or promotee officials. No doubt, some sort of training whether internal or through external sources is provided to such officials to expose them to specific industry/enterprise-related functions and processes. Grooming and succession planning concepts and processes are alien to them. It is mostly a sink or swim situation. And usually, the SEs rather than the individuals heading these units sink. This is witnessed in ample measures, in almost all the states. Lack of entrepreneurial skill, motivation and alienation could be the reasons.

PSUs, though manned by deputationists from the central cadres in early stages, have undergone a major change in respect of deployment of senior and top-level executives. Virtually, the process of manning top level positions has been institutionalized. Public enterprises selection board is one such institution which short-lists and recommends candidates to the government for placement in vacant slots. Training and development function is quite rampant in many PSUs to groom executives for various levels. In some cases even the practice of short-listing 'high performers' is being followed to groom them through mentoring, training and rotation. One Man Enterprises usually vanish after the death of the promoter unless, the progeny, especially sons step into the father's shoes and take the reins. In any case, these units have a limited life span. Thus, the concept of succession is not a debatable point. Sometimes the widows take over the units and run them for some time. The entire informal sector, or the tiny sector is managed more or less the same way.

Medium Size Enterprises usually grow organically out of the tiny or small sector units, or get established afresh by meeting regulatory threshhold norms, especially when such units are technical and professional cadres are deployed there. No specific and formal process of grooming and development is in vogue in these units. Offsprings of the entrepreneurs, if they opt to join these units, run them with the help of experienced people. These employees could operate as heads of the various functions or even run the factories yet, members of the family manage the enterprise till it goes beyond their capacity. Such enterprises abound in Patiala, Ludhiana, Amritsar and Jullundur in Punjab and even in Haryana.

A major industrial house in Punjab had to close down five factories and exit from that activity, when the siblings chose to stay out of the empire built by their father. Even though the remaining two units are still being managed well by the promoter with the help of professionals, yet their long-term survival could be at stake.

Large Enterprises are often plagued with the problem of succession, when either their siblings opt out of the family business or the promoter does not happen to have a son or a nephew or even a daughter to manage the business when he grows old.

Under the circumstances, it is imperative that when an enterprise grows to a particular size, it is listed on the stock exchange of the region and the various stakeholders are made to participate in the process of initiating the requisite succession planning measures through the professionals. This practice is quite rampant in MNCs and other large enterprises in advanced countries. This way, the causality rate of private enterprises will diminish considerably.

Nostalgic trips to my days with an MNC remind me of a well-articulated multi-dimensional grooming process of local executives to equip them to climb into the country Head position or at least No. 2 slot. This ensured a virtual corporate immortality through smooth succession.

Part II

CEOs' Universe

CHAPTER - 19

Crestfallen CEOs Scramble for Chastity Belt

In recent years corporates around the world seem to have been caught in a cobweb of vices of various types and dimensions. According to the Shastras and Hindu scriptures, lust, anger, greed, attachment and ego detract an individual from the path of sanity. Being victim of any one of the vices singly or in combination one could get derailed from the virtuous life course. Once an individual becomes a prisoner of vices it is difficult for him to think, act and perform in the right way. The behaviour undergoes a change and one gets mired in muck. The main victims of these vices are virtues like values, missions, noble goals and integrity one aspires to maintain and achieve in life.

The recent corporate shenanigans like trickery, deceit and scams are clear manifestations of misconduct of the CEOs, top executives and the various professionals like CAs, auditors and bankers. It is no wonder that after the unravelling of various scams, the US has lost its sparkle as an icon of market ideas. As for India, the less said the better as politicians and bureaucrats force corporates to deviate from the right course and bypass the laws. Not to mention leading the world the Indian corporates have not even come closer to the less endowed MNC corporates.

This way bubble era dreams of ever escalating stock prices have shattered. It is difficult to say whether the flurry of activities leading to formation of regulatory rules would ever revive the sagging morale of the community and the image of the CEOs of various corporations who have become slaves of short-term gyrations of the stock market.

A few examples from the corporate world like the public sector, private sector and the MNCs would illustrate the point.

Lust : In the earlier decades after India achieved independence most of the business was being managed by the MNCs, particularly the trading activity. The CEOs and high level executives would often employ lady secretaries in their offices. Some of the CEOs would get so involved that their vision would get confined to the office and they would hardly see anything beyond the secretary's legs. Even while going on a holiday, they would insist that their secretaries accompany them. Their lack of interest in the job and limited interaction with the market would affect their performance. Particularly, in the case of Indian executives employed in the MNCs, the main criteria according to their own perception about their capability was the capacity to hold liquor. Quite a few young executives in their early 30s and mid-30s lost their valuable lives because of excessive indulgence in wine and women. In some cases even marriages were on the rocks.

Anger : Some of the CEOs are so short-tempered that they become intolerant even at the very sight of their colleagues, customers and various suppliers and vendors. One of the CEOs in a private sector undertaking would often get so upset about minor issues that it would affect his faculties of taking correct decisions. A very senior executive in a public sector undertaking was a victim of his assumed competence and abilities. He did not have the patience to listen to the views and explanations of his junior colleagues and would often start shouting and trembling with rage within a few seconds of interaction with them. He was also a victim of his inflated ego which probably was due to his educational background as he had managed to secure the second position in the University at the postgraduate level. Thus ego combined with anger played havoc with the lives of his colleagues. This created ripples of unrest in the people above, below and around him and consequently he was made to part company with the organization.

Greed: This particular vice has virtually plagued the entire corporate world in the US, Japan, Germany and India. The recent disclosures about financial convulsions in the stock market and the miserable plight of millions of small investors is a clear manifestation of the corporate greed. Near home examples abound in the state and central public sector enterprises and even in the government where top level executives have played havoc with the public office and looted the society. CEOs and other high level functionaries are treating their position and power as licence for larceny. Some of the frauds have been rightly trapped by the CBI and put behind bars by the authorities.

Attachment: Materialism has almost sown the seeds of attachment to wealth in the corporate world. The more one has the more one craves for. No doubt, a minimal amount of attachment is essential for the normal run of life in society. Yet, once human behaviour attains disproportionate dimensions to the requisite quantum of attachment, matters go out of control and assume devilish proportions. It is, therefore, imperative that the tug of war between the vices and virtues does not result in the former dominating the latter.

Hence, the CEOs must strive to recover fast from the present traumatic situation and re-establish credibility with the corporate stakeholders through sincerity and intensity of purpose.

CHAPTER - 20

Relevance of Gandhian Values for Corporate CEOs

It is believed that the vision and values constitute the foundation of an organization. This is so as an organization is a micro system within the vast expanse of society. Since the survival of a society is based on the sustenance of values, the organization being a sub-system of the society has to respond to the value system of the society at large. Moreover, as the whole gamut of human activity constitutes an indivisible approach to social, economic, commercial and political situations, it is essential that the organizational man takes cognizance of this vital fact and crafts his responses accordingly. The corporates, therefore, cannot have the luxury of arrogant stances which seek to monopolize legitimacy.

Accepting this thesis as the basis of social phenomenon the person wielding power and authority has to ensure that he displays maturity in the use of power and respects the ego, ideas and the sentiments of the various stakeholders. In fact, he has to nurture his constituencies for the sake of growth and survival of his enterprises. He has to be clear about the context and the purpose for which the organization exists. He need not propitiate the individuals but treat them in a just and fair manner.

In the context of this premise, one may wish to dwell upon the values/principles which Mahatma Gandhi advocated for mankind and examine their relevance for the corporate chiefs. These values are truth, non-violence and universal brotherhood.

Truth - The element of truth forms the basis of integrity and morality which often constitues the subject of study and deliberations at different stages of life. Initially when an individual goes through the process of education, especially in the school and management institute, a lot of stress is given on the factor of ethics. In fact, starting from Harvard Business School almost every other reputed management school has included this subject in the curriculum of study. It is assumed that ethics has to underpin not only thinking but the actions of an individual in the organization as well as outside. Whether it is employees, vendors, the customers, shareholders or any other segment of the society who are affected directly or indirectly by the activities of the organization, have to be given a fair and just deal.

The coorporates have to conduct themselves in a transparent and responsible manner. This shows that the CEO must translate the spirit of truth in the ethical behaviour of its constituents. Even when he is under stress or is threatened by competition or misdemeanor of the rivals he should not deviate from the path of truth as it provides moral strength. May be somebody is able to supress the wrong doings for some time but eventually, the truth has to prevail as it has happened in the case of the recent unravelling of the various scams and scandals in the corporate realms in different countries including India. When a situation like this emerges, one really gets nonplussed and rues his action and behaviour which he might have displayed under the influence of greed or some other vicious designs.

Non-violence : Violence does not necessarily mean a violent physical action on the part of a powerful person to hurt, degrade or physically cause damage to a weaker person. In the corporate context, violence means outrageous action or arrogant behaviour on the part of the superior to subdue the subordinate or a person who is under his control and influence. In other words, it could mean bullying the other person to prove one's power and authority over him. Virtually, bullying is a part of transactional interaction, between the boss and his subordinate or any other constituent which has to depend for favours on the superior authority.

The violent action is usually performed in a subtle way so as to gain power from feeding human desperation. Usually, the most powerful person in any corporation is the chief executive who happens to hold immense control on the various segments of the organization. He can thus display brutal force to subjugate others to bring them to his point of view. He can even hide his own incompetence by blaming others for his inaction, follies and failures. He could bully a person in such a way that the object loses confidence in himself and becomes a victim of the nefarious situation caused by the subtle violence implicit in the behaviour of the boss.

The CEO has to realize that the violence in the work place affects not only the morale and mentality of a particular individual but it ravages the entire organization and the various other stakeholders. This practice could lead to a wider act of manipulation by each one to out manoeuvre the other either by bullying or browbeating. It is, therefore essential that the corporates do not take recourse to violent means in the conduct of their activities. No doubt at times the CEO has to take recourse to strong hand measures to check the activities of the miscreants.

Universal Brotherhood. In the socio-religious context brotherhood means love for mankind. In other words, it means doing to others what one would like to be done to oneself. In the corporate context, it could mean that CEOs have to empathize with the various stakeholders and the society. They have to show concern for the well-being of the people and participate in the various welfare activities to improve the social and economic lot of the people. The emphasis here is on the social responsibility of the corporates and their love and care not only for their customers but the society as a whole.

Even though customer relationship marketing (CRM) concept to some extent does mean that emphasis has to be given to the relationship aspect yet, the actual activity is usually confined to the relationship orientation and special care of the high value customers. It needs to be appreciated that this parochial approach has to be curbed in the general interest of the society, as the need of an individual for a product or a service could be highly relevant from the individual's point of view. This way the concept of universality in terms of brotherhood and a cordial relationship has to be given utmost importance. Incidentally, Gandhian values are equally relevant for the politicians and the bureaucrats not only symbolically but in action and delivery as they have to interact with the common man as a part of their routine activity.

CHAPTER - 21

Adherence to Vision and Values Could Restore CEOs' Charisma

The word charisma has its origin in Greek civilization and accordingly charisma sprngs from the ingrained personal traits like over-reaching ambition, unshakable confidence and the penchant for setting a personal example. This holds relevance for a person in any walk of life, say social, economic, political and business. It is so, as charisma has been defined as a divinely conferred gift or, the special spiritual power or personal quality that gives an individual influence or authority over a large number of people. Charisma could also be a special virtue of an office, function or position conferred on a person. A CEO being the organizational leader has to have the various qualities associated with the leader including the charismatic leader. But what is really debatable is whether charisma is an inalienable feature of the personality of an individual or if it vanishes from the personality under different circumstances.

It is a well-known fact that a particular individual who might have been immensely successful in a particular enviornment may feel inadequate in a different setting. This is so, as the various traits imbibed by him in a particular culture may not fit in a diverse cultural more. Besides, what is considered as ethical or moral may not be accepted as a part of the behaviour in an alien situation.

But what really baffles the mind is the fact whether, a particular strategy, philosophy, operational mode and policy which have ensured an individual's glowing success and smooth sailing thus far could really be the factors to be reckoned in the event of a slip or departure from the expected role behaviour. It has been observed that, even great leaders excepting perhaps the spiritual leaders of the various religions and spiritual-cum-social leaders like Mahatma Gandhi could really continue to operate on the basis of charisma of their personality. Often whether it is a CEO or, any other head of any institution which displays charisma and holds sway and influence over a large segment of employees, stakeholders and general public by virtue of the powers and authority vested in him due to the official position, could be robbed of this virtue at any point of time when he is unable to cope with the expectations held by the people about his role.

A few examples from the corporate world as also political arena could be highlighted to prove the thesis :

I. Mr. Ramani was appointed as Managing Director of a big public sector undertaking a few years ago. He was held in high esteem by the so-called charisma of his personality as also efficient performance of his role as a chief executive. He continued to hold his influence on the minds of the executives, trade union leaders and the bureaucrats for about two years at a stretch. Thereafter a minor slip on his part annoyed the people in power in the state bureaucracy. This affected his smooth functioning and resulted in strained relations with the state government. This further resulted in his loss of influence and confidence with his own executives and employees in the organization as most of them started questioning the legitimacy of his role as a CEO. This also resulted in drifting of authority from his position as a leader. Ultimately he got so fed up, that he requested the government for a transfer to some other place.

II. Rebecca Mark of Enron was considered to be a celebrity in the executive realms around the world. People claimed that the lady had a charismatic personality which enabled her to exert influence over the people both inside and outside the corporation. But later on when she was unable to resolve the conflicting issue with the state government of Maharashtra, people started losing faith in her charisma as an executive leader. Subsequently, with the collapse of Enron Corporation, the situation became still worse. In a situation like this, role dysfunctioning at the level of Rebecca and Malfeasance at the corporate level resulted in loss of face and faith in the community in the US and abroad.

III. Jawaharlal Nehru, a great charismatic leader of India who held sway over the destiny of the nation for a long time and was treated almost like God by the people, started losing his political influence after the 1962 war with China. The public started questioning the sanctity of the Panchsheel Treaty with China (which Nehru had entered into with Chou En-Lai on the basis of mutual understanding, trust and faith as the Chinese deceived India under the garb of mutual faith and sincerity.

IV. Sam Pitroda was considered to have a great charisma about his personality, especially when he was successful in piloting and implementing the Technology Mission in India with the blessings of the late Rajiv Gandhi, the Prime Minister of India. His influence over the bureacracy and the politicians was perhaps due to his closeness to the Prime Minister which element evaporated from the situation after the death of Rajiv Gandhi. Undoubtedly Sam Pitroda is doing well in his assigned role of CEO of World Tel yet his influene has declined owing to changed circumstances.

V. Lately Jack Welch, one of the most celebrated CEOs (GE) of the 20th century seems to have been put in an embarrassing position by his estranged wife about the hefty perks and facilities obtained by him at the time of retirement. No doubt the hapless shareholders and the public feel benumbed in bewilderment. Jack's pro-active gesture to surrender such bounties might restore his image of uprightness.

From the prevailing situation in the corporate world in the US, India and even Japan one can easily reckon that most of the CEOs who had risen to Elizabethan heights and rode the crest of glory by virtue of the so-called charisma of their personalities have succumbed to the process of dysfunctioning and malfeasance. CEOs thus need to take a lesson from the present tumult and turbulence in the market and ensure adherence to the vision, values and mission enshrined in their articles of association to regain their charisma and image.

CHAPTER – 22

CEOs' Throne : A Rocky Affair

One of the great philosophers of political science once remarked that life in the state of nature was nasty, brutish and short. Perhaps, it would be more apt in the case of a CEO, who is always exposed to the onslaughts of aspirants, rivals, peers and even bosses. No CEO could say with confidence that he would ever be able to survive till the expiry date of the tenure. This way, the shelf life of a CEO is shrinking menacingly year after year. Role expectation of the CEO by the various constituencies like the owners, board of directors, shareholders, financial institutions, banks and the various other stakeholders add further gravity to the situation. Manifestations of this phenomenon could be witnessed in any type of entity like a private enterprise, publicly owned company, PSU or an MNC. The only difference in these diverse enterprises would be that the actors and their tricks and techniques could be different.

Talking specifically about the various kinds of entities the scenario could be something like this :

Private Enterprise

While at the start up stage the promoters usually occupy the top slot, in course of time as the business grows and outlasts the youthful years of the initiator, a situation arises when he has to be succeeded by someone younger. In many situations, the first succession is usually smooth as the writ of the CEO holds sway. But subsequently, often, a war of attrition starts in the family circles. Those with more say and influence in the family start lobbying against the CEO and keep lighting fire under him. The situation could become so threatening for the CEO that he has to muster great courage to survive the assault. He may also take recourse to the various tricks in his armoury to confront the situation. The tricks could represent a continuum of expedients from divide and rule to the expulsion of the most likely aspirant or the trouble maker. Others, who may be less obnoxious yet dangerous could be exiled to distant locations. Yet others, who could not be banished from the corridors of power might be divested of important roles and made to stay dead on innocuous tasks. In the process, the CEO has to be vigilant all the time to obviate open as well as clandestine moves of the vested interests. However, when the CEO opts out, quits or is forced to vacate the chair his successor too has to continue to struggle to protect his turf assiduously.

Publicly Owned Enterprises

The CEO of such an enterprise has to guard his domain from the various stakeholders in addition to the members of the promoter's family. The most likely aspirants in this situation could be the executive directors whose evil eye remains focussed on the CEO's spot. The perks, power, halo, glory, package, prestige and influence which the CEO enjoys sometimes blind the aspirant EDs about their inadequacy and unsuitability and propels them to take recourse to politics and other odious means to tarnish the image of the CEO, defame him and destabilize his position. Other aspirants from the various constituencies like independent directors, major shareholders or even retired bureaucrats nominated or placed on the board could also stake their claims and get involved in the internecine war for angling support to achieve their mission. Thus, the CEO who usually feels lonely at the top often feels insecure and vulnerable to the malicious designs and uncontrolled ambition of the these players. Under the circumstances, the energies of the CEO get dissipated and survival on the job even till the completion of the contracted tenure becomes a nightmare.

Public Sector Undertakings

PSUs were havens of security till some time ago (perhaps even now) for the various executives below the top Cradle to grave was considered to be the duration of job tenure as no one ever lost the job on the basis of inefficiency. In fact, models of inefficiency could be found in abundance in PSUs Centre or State. SEs would rather excel central PSUs in this regard. However, the poor CEO has to be on his toes as his head is on the block all the time. "Damocle's sword" hangs perennially on his head and a minor slip could alienate the powers that be and cut short his tenure prematurely. The additional risk is also posed by the GMs or Eds who might aspire for the CEO's slot. They could go to any length to malign the image of the boss with gay abandon and cause him sleepless nights. The usual tricks employed by them are in the shape of lobbying with the directors of the board, trade union leaders, colleagues, politicians and the bureaucrats. The CEO is thus in constant danger of being trapped in the cobweb so woven around him. As such, the CEO of a PSU has to be an extremely shrewd person to keep the evil elements at bay. At this level, it is the efficiency rather than inefficiency and result orientation which makes enemies and offers an opportunity to the rivals and aspirants for politicking and maligning. If nothing works at least anonymous letters to the vigilance and CBI could cause anxiety to the CEO all the time. He has to adopt defensive postures to escape the radar screen of pernicious queries of these agencies. Thus the Grand Mughals (CEOs) of PSUs of yesteryears have to remain eternally vigilant to save their tenure. That is why people in the corporate world find it much more difficult to survive as a CEO than to attain this position. Yet the lure never diminishes, even when it means enjoying just 15 minutes' fame.

CHAPTER – 23

Why CEOs Feel Lonely at the Top

It is usually believed that loneliness creates strain on the mind of a person. It is also a well-known fact that one seeks solitude for concentration and deep thinking. Corporates have also realized from experience that the process of strategy planning requires calm, quiet, and an uninterrupted environment. Hence a congenial ambience and quietude constitute the necessary pre-conditions for effective functioning of a CEO. It is, therefore, a strange paradox that still every single executive who has the talent and ambition to move up the corporate pyramid aspires to achieve the position of a CEO in the shortest possible time. This is so, despite the fact that the upward journey to the corner room is full of thorny patches. The process is so arduous that one could even have a feeling of burnout while traversing this course.

Probably the perception about perks and other benefits in terms of authority, status, influence, name, fame, ego, satisfaction and attainment of self-actualization provide the trade off between perceived gains and the loss for joining the perilous race to the top. Moreover, it is one of the most difficult and challenging tasks for the Directors and the retiring CEO to find the so-called super star who can effectively fill the chair of the Chief Executive. Virtually, the CEO is the embodiment of collective aspirations of the employees shareholders, members of the Board, suppliers, vendors, clients, politicians, co-professionals, corporate associations and the community at large. This fulfils the wish of an individual to have arrived.

Apparently, till an individual has hit the CEO's spot every thing looks rosy, glamorous and attractive. Yet, the hype created by the environment, innate ambition of the individual and the expectations of the stakeholders about the lofty role are negated by the stark reality of loneliness and stress at the top.

The various factors which force a CEO to remain aloof could be enumerated as follows :

Strategy Planning

Strategy planning is the process which requires total concentration for the creativity and stimulation of the mind to design the right modes and methods for the growth and survival of an enterprise. This exercise requires deep analysis of the facts and figures skilful evaluation of the various alternatives for working out a viable strategy. In case the mission of the organization is to attain and maintain number one position in the market, the process would entail a comprehensive exercise to evolve an effective strategy. The process could be still more arduous if the enterprise is operating on the global scale. Hence any interruption or disturbance could cause a major deviation from the predetermined course.

Competition : Competition has become so intense and perpetual that the CEO has to remain on the alert all the time. Whether the challenge is posed by others locally or foreign enterprises one has to act like an astute player. Competition is virtually a chess game and requires full concentration of the mind for every single move to outwit the opponent.

Rivalry : Corporate rivalry is a fact of life whether it is the process of seeking visibility and staying power in one's business circle, association or other similar institutions. The mind has to be constantly agile to outmanoeuvre the rivals who may be striving for similar distinction. This no doubt requires a certain amount of confidentiality even from close associates.

Favour Seekers : The CEO is always exposed to the temptations of the various constituents to get closer to him to seek favours. The CEO has therefore to be careful and selective in extending the hand of friendship to various people. The closer one happens to be to the CEO the more he is likely to exploit him in his lighter moments and moods. Whether it is a PSU, a private entity, an MNC or any other institution the story is the same.

Decision-Making: Making correct and objective decisions is the most important function of a CEO. Hence decision-making should not be influenced by anyone. Easy accessibility and informality has to be guarded zealously and assiduously by the chief executive except from those needed for consultation and help. In fact, the CEO has to be careful even from his elbow guys lest they feed him filtered and motivated information. Even when he has confided to certain people hard facts need to be kept under wraps.

Self-Security : Individual security of the CEO has gained seriousness because of the constant threat to his person and position from the aggrieved elements, mercenaries, kidnappers, the underworld dons and others. Thus he cannot rely on everyone and has to defend himself from them.

Status : Especially in such a place where an exclusive township has been developed around an enterprise, the CEO has to be careful about his movements as he could be easily identified and singled out. He has, therefore, to avoid free mixing with the people except in the case of a small organization where the number of employees is too small to be formal. This is so in the case of start ups, SMEs and other small service organizations.

Family Life : The CEO has to maintain work life balance in view of the constant demand on his time by the various stakeholders and institutions. Time being short with all these commitments, he has to maintain formality with the people to avoid encroachment on his family life. Also, as there is tremendous pressure on his mind and body, he needs time for relaxation and exclusive socialization.

All the above factors put together make the life of a CEO rather isolated and lonely.

CHAPTER – 24

Changing Context of CEOs' Development

Anyone actively associated with the top level management programmes would have observed that CEOs or the heads of various corporate bodies variously designated as GM, ED, Director, President, Chairman and so on usually participate actively at seminars, conferences and conventions on international meets. Irrespective of the fact whether such events or programmes focus on basic topics like leadership, communication, team building, commitment building, trust building and so on or relate to the various skills like conceptual, inter-personal and administrative or, deliberations coverage on general awareness among CEOs regarding the impact of technology, abrupt change, emergent social issues and corporate citizenship, the extent of participation and involvement remains fairly adequate. The urge being to enhance professional shelf life and keep up with recent trends by embracing novel management fads that debut on the corporate catwalk. This also helps to remain distinct and not become extinct.

Over time, the management ideologues or the corporates themselves are seeking exposure to subjects like corporate mission, vision, values, purpose and strategy in this regard.

With the passage of time, the focus is gradually shifting to contemporary corporate and social issues. This could relate to the process of growth and development of business in the face of competition from the locals and MNCs. As expansion of the various enterprises is mostly being made through the process of joint ventures, acquisitions, takeovers and mergers, increased emphasis is being placed on issues like strategic alliance, negotiating skills, due diligence and such other processes like restructuring, smooth transition, cultural assimilation, ethnic concerns, reorientation in policies, systems and strategy. HRD aspects having a deep impact on executive psyche in terms of position, powers, rank and compensation also figure prominently in such discussions with a view to find viable solutions.

Yet other important areas which have assumed major significance in the last one decade or so relate to the process of preventive measures through strategy formulation and laying down of action guidelines to reduce the impact of barbaric terrorist activity in the area of operation of various enterprises. Associated with the concern and anxiety for such disruptive onslaughts the subject of crisis management, disaster management, rehabilitation of the various stakeholders including employees on account of the carnage perpetrated by such unforeseen acts of vandalism has assumed great significance. The various other topics like formulation of policies to check discrimination and bias on the basis of caste, creed and sex, management of diversity, etc. are also being discussed at these seminars. Participation of women, handicapped persons, other deprived sections of society and checkmating discrimination on the basis of colour and social background assume importance depending on the intensity of an issue at a particular juncture.

In addition to the above, the various other topics which are rising high in the scale of concern of top management and CEOs in particular, relate to the effective corporate governance, challenge of globalization, demolition of national barriers in the area of international trade, movement of manpower (both high level executives and skilled workers), flow of funds across national borders and putting up of production and manufacturing units in other countries with the procurement of plant and equipment from different parts of the world. Marketing of products and services, especially in other countries to the various destinations in the world are engaging the attention of the people associated with the development of top level corporate executives. Hence CEOs need constant exposure to the various concepts, practices, techniques and strategy in all these spheres. Ethics having been dilated upon ad nauseam without much impact on CEOs' (quite a few) attitude and dealings need not form the subject of deliberations as, enough is enough.

It may be pertinent to point out that some of the CEOs do hesitate to participate actively in the various seminars and conferences held within the country except when invited to inaugurate such events in the capacity of a chief quest. Yet, whenever, opportunities arise in the economically advanced countries like the US, Japan, Europe or even China (especially in the last few years), they prefer to participate themselves or their siblings (prospective CEOs) in the case of family owned companies rather than nominating other executives to such seminars or conventions.

Considering the fact, that the process of learning has to be a lifelong affair it is vital for the CEOs to keep moving along the learning curve lest, the process of their growth and development gets plateaued. Anyone who is unable to cope with the ever evolving pattern of development of self, stakeholders and the organization as a whole must avail himself of the opportunity to drop out and take recourse to an elemental life away from the corporate trappings and lure of the corner room.

CHAPTER - 25

How CEOs, Behave and Operate

During the course of my working career of a little over four decades I have had occasion to work and interact with several CEOs in PSUs, MNCs and the private sector. The first encounter happened to be with the Chief Accountant (CEO) of a departmental undertaking dealing with the rehabilitation of displaced persons. He had a laidback style of work as was often the case in government undertakings in the 1950s. Usually bound by governmental policies and procedures, he had prescribed checks and controls for the various activities. Some time the young and flamboyant employees would bypass the rules yet, would usually follow the path of custom. The next chief happened to be a bully. On his very sight an employee would turn his back to him yet, sir him to death when face-to-face.

In the MNC, out of the three CEOs, two were Indians and one an Englishman. One of the Indian CEOs was rather stiff-necked and a believer in strict discipline. He was hardly accessible even to the senior managers unless called to his office. Being a trading company, executive performance was judged on achieving product-wise sale targets. The second CEO happened to be British. He was open and accessible. Virtually, a hail-fellow type. Though his towering figure inspired awe yet, he commanded respect and trust from the executives and staff alike. The third CEO was from a royal Indian family and exhibited all the traits of a prince. Though kind and accommodating yet, quite demanding on the job. He held the highest position in the country in the MNC ever assigned to an Indian. No wonder, during his regine the MNC had captured 65 per cent of the oil market in the country.

In PSUs the encounter was extended to a span of 22 years with several CEOs. The first one was a Christian and God-fearing individual. Being an engineer by education and experience, he had a knack and eye for detail. While having full control on the technical aspects, he gave due regard to the professionals for their advice and cooperation. The next chief had a long stint with defence production and, as such, was a great stickler for rules. Being shrewd and conscious of vigilance implications, he would obtain signatures of the various concerned departmental heads on various proposals to ensure their commitment before according approval. Checks and controls in the form of pre-audit, concurrent audit and post-audit had to be carried out meticulously. He would mostly depend on executives drawn from the defence services and others from central services on deputation. Rather impatient and over committed to targeted completion of the project, he would go all out to acquire the requisite resources.

The next CEO had a long stint in the steel industry. He was a man of high morals, discipline and dedication. Even though procedure-oriented, yet he believed in speedy and timely action through delegation, autonomy and prudent use of powers by the executives. A highly respected and awe-inspiring individual. A simple call from him to an executive would stir him to instant action. The next chief came from an ordinance department of defence services He had no previous experience in industry. A very honest, straightforward and informal individual. Being unequal to the task he withdrew promptly. However, on return to his organization was pushed up to the highest spot. His successor was a man with long experience in the steel industry. He was fully confident of his capabilities and the challenge of the job. His style displayed a type of careful carelessness about the various problems and issues. No one could bluff him about technical and non-technical issues owing to his familiarity with the folklore of the industry. Despite the labour unions' impatience with him, he had a long tenure on the job.

A tall, hefty and handsome man with a long stint in steel industry became the next CEO. He encouraged informal discussions with the senior management and others at various levels and virtually ran a paperless office. Hardly ever had he dictated a letter except when communicating with the outside agencies in unavoidable circumstances. During his time, the project made profits for the first time despite a long strike by the labour unions immediately on his joining. He had to carry the burden of his predecessors for the labour problems. He was a likable person and would inspire instant confidence in the people by his open and frank disposition. The man who took over from him was again from the steel industry with sound background in designs. Though he did not have much exposure at the corporate level for managing huge projects yet, soon was bale to command the situation by virtue of his intelligence, instant adaptability and confidence. He was almost a one minute manager and would not mind appreciating or firing his executives as the occasion warranted.

The writer's last encounter was with the CEOs of the private sector. Being low on budget and resources the first CEO of an 'opinion poll' organization was rather thrifty. He was virtually a lean counter. All the powers centred in him. He would often cross-check facts and figures from various sources before arriving at a conclusion.

The CEO of an engineering enterprise located in Madhya Pradesh and having 7 to 8 units (forging, casting, engineering) occupied the position by virtue of the family hierarchy. Though lavish in his living style, he had very simple food habits. He was quite informal with the consultants but formal with his own executives and staff. His attention was constantly focused on the bottomline and growth.

The author's next contact was with an industrial house in northern India. The CEO was an engineer by education. He had a five-year stint with the government before embarking on an entrepreneurial career. A unique blend of personality of a PSU CEO and private sector top executive, a quick decision-maker and a confident person. At times he would get rough with the executives for making mistakes or, for not taking enough initiative.

He was a one minute manager. Like a good entrepreneur he would constantly watch the bottomline and performance of the executive and the other staff.

Thus even in the same sector, i.e. public, private or MNC the CEOs could have different styles yet, would frequently run the organization effectively and successfully. Indeed a kaleidoscopic pattern of styles. Awareness of CEOs' style really helps one to adjust and adopt.

CHAPTER – 26

CEOs' Cultural Orientation Aids Effective Decision-Making

The success of a corporation depends normally on the type of decisions the CEOs make. Decisions are often classified in two broad categories–structured and unstructured. Decisions could be further classified into strategic, managerial and operational. The quality of decisions depends to a great extent on the physical, mental, emotional and spiritual capacity of a CEO. Besides it also depends on the combination of faith, facts and gut feel. The other factors which really distinguish a highly successful CEO from others relate to his penchant for the participation of people in the decision-making process. It is so, as a successful CEO is supposed to possess the traits of a talented individual, a team member, a competent manager, an effective leader and a combination of humility and professional will.

Further, what aids the decision-making process is the relentless pursuit of a particular concept and strategy. Also knowledge of one big thing or an idea rather than knowing a little bit of too many things helps the process of effective decision-making. Yet another factor, which aids the process of effective decision-making could be the application of carefully selected and pioneered options. Moreover, the culture of discipline in the organization where, a combination of disciplined people, disciplined thoughts and disciplined action obtain, helps not only in making viable decision but also in their effective implementation. Incidentally, the discipline of the people and their thoughts and actions eliminate the need for hierarchy, bureaucracy and elaborate controls which ensure speedy result-oriented implementation of decisions.

This way, the combination of culture and values of a

CEO distinguish him from the rest of the flock in spearheading his organization to success through sound and healthy decisions.

The surveys, studies and research carried out by the academicians and students of management and practitioners have led us to believe that a gut feel and hunch are often taken recourse to by the successful chief executives in making decisions. Gut instincts are given emphasis because of the fact that, they represent a sum total of millions and millions of experiences which the CEOs acquire over a period of time. Virtually, a gut feel is the outcome of intuitive skills which often involves the entire mind. Over time, the intuition and judgement represent the sort of analysis which gets frozen into the mind.

Despite the fact that most of these things are known to the CEOs and they also endeavour to follow the theories evolved and the models developed by the experts in this regard, yet the real life stories offer a mixed scenario with regard to the process of decision-making.

A few examples from the corporate world would help to elucidate this thesis in a clear manner.

Mr. Rana (name changed to protect identity), the country head of an MNC would often spend considerable time in obtaining facts and figures from all possible sources he could access. He would also call the senior executives to his office for collecting further information and soliciting their opinions on the specific issues. The process of consultations could last several days on certain occasions. Despite all this drill when the question of taking decisions would arise, he would feel shaky and diffident. He would often waver in his mind and get confused. The outcome would usually be disappointing as the actions would get delayed. No doubt, he had to be replaced by another individual and reverted to the earlier position. Meantime, to overcome the situation the top management constituted a committee of management to take timely decisions.

Mr. Rawal, a CEO in a public sector undertaking, believed in taking structured decisions. As such, various proposals emanating from the lower levels in the hierarchy were screened and processed for recommendation to the next higher level in the hierarchy. Ultimately, a thoroughly screened and structured proposal with all the facts and figures in summarized form would go to him for the final decision. At times, this procedure did delay the process of decision-making, yet the outcome was usually foolproof and appropriate to the situation. He had further classified decisions into two categories, i.e. the ones having a large area of impact and others with a limited operational impact on the working of the organization. Obviously, decisions having a wide corporate impact were studied in greater detail and depth.

In a private enterprise, the CEO often depended on his gut feel, intuition and judgement. In other words, this was a situation where faith, facts and emotions played a vital role in making decisions. This approach represented the sum total of his experiences about the working of an enterprise. His approach was almost similar to most of the CEOs who often take recourse to such processes before arriving at viable decisions.

Such CEOs are really able to contribute to the growth, prosperity and success of their organizations. They could be described as decision leaders in the corporate world by virtue of this distinct potential and multiple capability.

CHAPTER – 27

CEOs' Role During Different Stages of an Enterprise

A study on the subject of the role and responsibility of a CEO would be more purposeful if a distinction is made between the promoter CEO and professional chief executive. While the promoter CEO's association with an enterprise is lifelong that of a professional could be tenure-based. The promoter CEO is more involved at different stages like conceptual, planning, construction or building, operation, expansion and growth and decline. The various phases an enterprises has to pass through could be likened to the life course of a human being, namely birth, adolescence, maturity, decline and death. Further each stage and phase is characterized by a combination of diverse factors like structure, geography and competition.

At the initial stage an intensive process of thinking, planning, evaluating, assessing and conceptualizing is involved. The selection of a particular project, a product and services to be offered depends to a great extent on the business scenario like the entry barriers, competitive landscape, availability of capital and other resources. The vision and values also impinge on the whole process. Once a particular project or product has been selected the focus of activity gets shifted to selection of site and technology, infrastructure development, access to the market and the related issues subject to clearance of the proposal from the controlling powers.

Now the CEO may look for outside help from consultants or experts. After short-listing consultants, the CEO has to obtain information about the availability of various resources like plant and equipment, finance and expertise. At this stage neither the role of a CEO nor that of other associates is well-defined. The process rather requires articulation and insightfulness. Once the project report and the basic framework is ready the area of activity becomes more specific and focussed. This is the time for determining the time schedule of activity of the project. An effort is also made to build a team of competent specialists to lead, guide and undertake activities in their respective fields. The process of decision-making remains unstructured and overlapping as necessary delegation could be made only when things take concrete shape.

The situation portrayed is more relevant for green field projects or activities requiring the development of a vast geographical network in the country as most of the activities could be out sourced or assigned to contractors and consultants. Along side a major area of concern for the CEO could be building the requisite organization and manning the various functions and activities as the project gets closer to the operation stage. During the course of operation, or normal running of an enterprise, things start taking definite shape and the process gets underway to put in place the strategy, the systems, the structure and requisite man power. Requisite delegation and specific roles also get defined for the various functions and suitable mechanisms in terms of high and low level controls too get installed. Necessary monitoring and feedback system too gets into the functional mode.

Moreover, the process of the hardware and software maintenance also gets initiated. The CEO assumes the definite role of a leader and initiates due process of communication, motivation, morale building, trust building, involvement and participation of employees through coaching, mentoring, training and other requisite processes. In other words, the CEO assumes the role of man management and his interpersonal skills get into full play. To promote the product and the services CEO has also to ensure that a fair image is projected of the organization. In fact the CEO being the public face of the organization has to build the CEO brand to create confidence in the various stakeholders. Incidentally, the reputation of a corporation as evident from different business houses of Reliance, Tatas, Birlas, Modis, Coca Cola, IBM, GE and many others depends on the reputation of the CEO.

Over time, either when the market scenario undergoes a change or the organization faces some crisis or upheaval due to some social, economic or political developments, the role of the CEO assumes a different dimension. A sort of nervous and hasty reaction to the situation could lead to patchwork and short cut measures. The situation becomes worse when the organization is plagued by scams, scandals and stock market blow outs. Maintaining the market share, cash flow, reliability of the accounting system, building confidence amongst stakeholders and other such ameliorative measures draw attention of the CEO. This causes a serious strain on his mind and body. The top most priority at this stage being the revival of the whole situation. If unable to manage, the CEO either opts out or is thrown out.

In the case of family-owned enterprises as is the case in India or even abroad, it is generally assumed that the first generation CEO builds the organization in the face of all the challenges and uncertainties, the second generation CEO consolidates the expansion and diversification brought about by him or his predecessor and by the time the third generation CEO steps into the business, his role becomes complex and unstructured as the organization starts disintegrating and withering by virtue of family feuds, separation and clash of opinions and interests.

As such the role of the CEO keeps changing at every stage and phase of an organization.

CHAPTER - 28

Skills and Techniques Relevant for the Success of CEOs

A study of the corporate phenomena shows that the success or failure of a CEO depends on the use of skills and techniques relevant for business. It is also gathered from experience that skills and techniques have a specific context. In fact the contemporary situation often dictates the use of a particular skill or a technique. While the various skills like the conceptual skill, communicative skill, interpersonal skill, administrative skill (which are often considered as generic skills for managers), IT skill, and other mental skills are essential for the effectiveness of a CEO, the techniques on the other hand, have direct relevance to the type of technology, market conditions, nature of competition and its dimension, specific sector of activity like public, private and MNC and the social, economic and political environment. Thus skills and techniques operate in unison.

This hypothesis is based on abstract skills and techniques relevant for the success of CEOs as highlighted in the award winning papers selected from more than 150 papers invited by the Centre for Public Sector Studies and Parliamentary Forum on Public Enterprises from executives in government and PSUs in 1984. While most of the paper writers emphasized use of skills and techniques like application of new concepts and practices, planning, organizing and flexibility, scanning of environment, understanding and correct judgement and rational decision-making entrepreneurial skills, initiative, environment assessment, creation of congenial internal environment, coordination, collective endeavour, motivation, leadership, participation, innovation, system orientation, tactfulness, team work, social participation, competence and combination of skills none of the concepts, theories and techniques like TOM, TPM,

CRM, KM, ISO 9000, Benchmarking, Re-Engineering, ERM, JIT, supply chain management, customer service and strategic alliance advocated these days for CEOs' support and involvement were mentioned in these papers. This summary reflects a bias for PSUs and the contemporary skills and techniques valid for their operating philosophy and raison *de'tre*

This shows that while most of the skills have a fundamental relevance for the CEOs, the techniques are context-specific. For instance, skills in managing diversity in the religious, cultural, and national characteristics in the context of global and multicultural coordination have assumed great relevance these days. Moreover, the process of growth of organizations through mergers and acquisitions has lent further credence to the application of requisite techniques. Negotiating skills, adeptness at strategic alliances, handling global exposure and the process of effective corporate governance have assumed great importance. It is therefore, imperative that a CEO makes a judicious selection of skills and techniques to be applied in a particular situation.

To cap it all, the CEO must have vision, an innovative mind, entrepreneurial and leadership qualities, emotional maturity and a knack for taking calculated risks. He must also develop and install certain mechanisms to measure the performance of his colleagues and that of his own. The response to the various challenges and problems should reflect deep analysis of a situation rather than a prompt superficial stock response. To forestall future trouble and failure it is essential to assess the coping strategy and the response capability of the corporation to the fast changing situation and sudden exigencies arising out of unpredictable developments.

The present local and global corporate operations which are marred by frequent scams, frauds, and other financial manipulations need to be handled carefully and defaults addressed rather aggressively. This will help avoiding further business misbehaviour by the CEO's colleagues, rivals and the various institutions on which he has to depend for the survival of the corporation as also his own.

It may be pertinent to point out, that the present scenario both in the public and private sector has thrown up challenges of an almost similar type and dimension which were particularly absent from the concern of CEOs of PSUs in the earlier decades. As both the PSUs and private corporations have to face tough competition from the MNCs and other local eivals they have to reorient their approach in terms of skills and techniques relevant for the successful operation of business.

CHAPTER - 29

How CEOs Manage Their Time

It has been observed that each level in the corporate hierarchy has certain unique characteristics. This aspect has a particular relevance for the level of a CEO. A major distinction between the lowest level in the hierarchy and the highest job is, that, while the former is represented by regular routine activities the job of a CEO is marred by discontinuities. At times, this could dissipate the energies of a CEO responding to the various demands mentally and physically. The time spent and the attention devoted to a particular activity or an issue may be of as short a duration as 10 seconds. It would, therefore, be appropriate to analyse the various activities a CEO has to perform and the type of interruptions which cause discontinuities.

Since the time available to all the human beings including the CEO is of a limited nature, it may be instructive to find out as to how the CEO of a major corporation or an undertaking employing as many as 20 lakh employees could manage his time effectively. During the course of informal discussion with the chairman of one of the largest undertakings of the country it transpired, that he was rather unsure as to how most of the CEOs coped with their responsibilities in the limited time available during the day. He even suggested to the writer that whether, a study could be undertaken to observe his activities for a week or so, to find out as to how he spent his time on various tasks. Incidentally, mostly people have vague perceptions about the time spent on a particular activity, unless a detailed study is done for the various activities performed during the day, the week, the fortnight, or a month against an accurate time scale. On his insistence, the study was done. The result of the observations showed that certain activities consumed much more time than others yet deserved less time. Besides phone calls, unexpected urgent faxes, e-mail, important visitors, emergencies and unenvisaged problems caused frequent disruptions. Some of the following factors may help to illustrate as to how CEOs manage their time.

Office Management : Effective management of time by a CEO depends on how he manages his office. Some of the CEOs take the assistance of their private secretaries, technical assistants, staff officers and other experts. Thus, various proposals coming to a CEO are referred to his TA, SO or PA as the case may be. After due scrutiny and study, and soliciting necessary information from the divisional heads or others who moot such proposals, the final summarized version is put up to the CEO for his consideration. This saves the CEO's time to a great extent.

The importance of the role of a PA could be imagined from the appraisal and the confidential reports given by a particular CEO to his PA. In one particular situation, when the PA of this CEO was subsequently placed under the writer, it was later revealed that the CEO had praised this individual in glowing terms and recorded on his confidential reports year after year that he would not have been able to operate so efficiently and effectively without his PA. He rewarded him with fast spurs for his stellar performance on the job. Though it appeared ridiculous to the writer in the first instance but later it transpired that the PA would have definitely offered a great support to the CEO in managing his time schedule.

Efficient Systems: One of the CEOs with whom the writer had a close encounter had a very efficient way of functioning. He had issued instructions to the divisional heads and others down the executive hierarchy to process proposals in such a manner that the case analysis, the comments of the executive and final recommendations at his level were recorded in a clear and concise manner before the proposal travelled to the next higher level. This way, the CEO would ultimately get a thoroughly screened proposal with specific recommendations from the divisional heads seeking his approval.

Dak Disposal: The number of cases or documents going upto the CEO could result in a big pile during the day. Hence, most of them priortize the proposals in order of their importance and immediacy. Initially, this could be done by the various members of staff in the CEO's office. Subsequently, depending on the nature of a proposal the CEO could record various comments like approved, not approved, please discuss, please review and put up please talk to me on phone, kindly bring executives from other divisions for discussion in my office after seeking a suitable time from the PA, please put up a proposal on my return from tour, or simply record seen and so on and dispose of the file.

Some of the CEOs, who have to undertake frequent tours often dispose of the routine mail while travelling in the company's plane or even public transport. Incidentally, it may be interesting to know that CEOs often keep their tables clean.

Community Affairs: Almost every CEO has some social responsibility to perform. But the CEOs of large corporations have to respond to the community affairs much more frequently and spend considerable time on various events. Such demands often arise from the politicians, bureaucrats, social organizations and other constituencies. Besides vendors, supplier and clients too demand a fair share of the CEO's time. To cope with the situation CEOs often take recourse to delegation of authority. For instance, petty politicians, bureaucrats and others could be tackled at lower levels like divisional and departmental heads or even the PA or TA of the CEO. Likewise, suppliers and vendors and other small clients could be tackled by the various executives in the company. However, the CEO has to be somewhat judicious and meticulous in dealing with the media, important politicians, bureaucrats and clients. Time has to be allocated for meetings and discussions with these constituencies. Normally PAs and TAs of even divisional heads assist the CEO in laying down priorities unless the matter requires instant attention.

Unions and Subordinates: The labour unions often claim considerable time and attention of the CEO, especially in PSUs.

He usually tackles the situation by appointing committees at the shop floor level, HOD and divisional head level and his own where, relevant issues could be discussed and tackled. Ultimately, the secret of effective time management by a CEO lies in the fact that he confines his focus judiciously and selectively to activities requiring a corporate level look. Besides, he must allow his subordinates to manage their time by being accessible without making them wait endlessly outside his cabin. Knowledge and use of electronic gadgets would also save his own and others' time and labour.

CHAPTER - 30

CEOs' Remuneration : A Contentious Issue

Pay scale structure for the blue collar or even white-collar workers is usually based on wage evaluation studies done for the representative jobs in an enterprise or the industry as a whole. This practice was quite prevalent in the initial stages when the country (India) was going in for industrialization. Systematic and scientific studies were often conducted in the public sector enterprises in this regard. For instance, 350 or so jobs were analysed and evaluated in the steel industry at the time of formulation of wage structure in the various steel units. TISCO too participated in these studies for designing the pay scale structure of the workers. Once the structure was established and hierarchy designed, all subsequent exercises in this regard for the new enterprises would adapt their scales with minor adjustments in the fixed or variable component of pay. However, some modification also depended on the various factors like level of education, training needs, responsibility, complexity and skill-mix.

Even when some of the factors involved in job evaluation of the worker category were relevant for the executive cadres namely, the level of education, experience, skill composition, etc., yet other important aspects like the nature and type of decisions to be made, decision load, impact area of decisions, time dimension of decisions, span of control, informed judgement, competence and so on were also considered for deciding the compensation package at different levels. The main factors of differentiation relevant for the various levels were whether, it was simply a point of cross over, coordination level or a decision point. These concepts provided the basis of comparison in the various enterprises either handling similar processes, products and technology or even dissimilar practices and patterns.

Pay scale structure so evolved was further punctuated by the aspect of number of levels in the hierarchy. The size, scope and complexity which normally govern the level of responsibility, authority and accountability of a senior executive were considered contextual to decide the category of an enterprise. Incidentally, in the case of public sector undertakings, the various enterprises were classified in four categories like A, B, C and D. In such an instance, the CMD of a D grade PSU could be considered at par with the general manager of an 'A' grade entity for the purpose of pay scale and other remunerations. However, the extent of gap in monetary terms was taken as the limiting factor for the highest paid executive, i.e. CEO with that of a worker at the lowest level in a PSU. Perhaps, a ratio of 10 : 1 has been considered appropriate for this purpose in India.

Another limiting factor for the ceiling was the package available to the hightest functionaries in the central government. The norms are rather variable in the various countries in the socialist and the capitalist realms like in Russia the emoluments gap between the workers and Russia (earlier USSR) and USA respectively. While the Chief Executive could be in the ratio of 1:4, in case of USA this gap could be phenomenal, i.e. 1:100 to 400/500. Hence a comparison would be just absurd and far-fetched.

Talking specifically about the remuneration or compensation of a CEO, various additional factors which normally come into play are the agency who has to decide the issue of remuneration, consideration for the going rates in the market, scarcity of talent, track record of the candidate, reputation in the market place and the community and the contacts with the legislatures, bureaucrats and other important persons who have substantial impact on the working of an enterprise. Other factors which also have relevance in this regard, could be the level of profitability, value of the stock and its appreciation, dividend generated for the shareholders, returns to the Banking Companies, financial institutions and others who are actively or otherwise affected by the results of an enterprise.

Whereas, the Schedule 13 of the Company Act has recently revised the various slabs for the purpose of payment of total emoluments including perks to the Chief Executive of a loss making unit, in the case of public sector undertakings a fixed pay scale structure generally is the deciding factor. According to the slab system, the minimum emoluments of the CEO of a publicly owned company with an effective capital of Rs. 1 crore are Rs. 75,000 per month, the maximum emoluments payable to a CEO of an enterprise with an effective capital of more than Rs. 100 crore is Rs. 2,00,000 per months. Factually, invisible means could boost this sum 5/6 times to meet social expectations. However, for a profit-making undertaking depending on the size and volume of activity and the profitability of an enterprise, the emoluments of a CEO could be much more in the shape of fixed pay, variables and commission not exceeding 5 per cent of the profits. Stock option returns could be reckoned additionally. Incidentally, compensation analysts feel that even performance pay ought to be contingent on a threshhold level of corporate performance. As reported in the media recently, the gross annual emoluments of the Chairman of Reliance group, Lt. Mr. Dhirubhai Ambani worked out to Rs. 9 crore. And for his two sons, remunerations vary from 7 to 8 crore per annum.

In the case of various large enterprises in USA or MNCs, the level of compensation of a CEO could far exceed even the widest imagination of the people associated with industry in India, even in large publicly owned companies like Tatas, Birlas and so on. In some cases, to circumvent the company law provision as also to escape criticism from the various stakeholders its service package is trimmed. But the post-retirement packet has been so formulated that the regular pension and other perks like club membership, provision of limousine with a chauffear, free accommodation with regular maintenance, foreign trips, lodging and boarding in luxury hotels and even free travel benefits virtually mean a far more glorious life after death. This may or may not have any relationship with the future prospects for growth or survival of an enterprise. Thus general debate about the appropriateness of a CEO's package or emoluments will continue to occupy the mind space of the shareholders of an enterprise, the directors, other stakeholders and the community at large for times to come. Who would not appreciate this type of lifestyle and heaven-like comforts on earth ?

CHAPTER - 31

Ceiling on CEOs' Remuneration : A Never Ending Debate

The subject of determing the package of a CEO has been under consideration for a long time. At times the issue comes under a sharp focus, especially, when some sort of incongruities are observed in the system, or there is a cry from the public and other concerned agencies. However, despite endless debates and the views expressed by the people held in high esteem in the country, no conclusive proposition has emerged.

It may be worthwhile going back to the previous era in this regard. Some time around the late 1970s, the Janata government in India came up with a proposal to put a ceiling on the remuneration of top management. Accordingly, discussions and debates were held at various fora in the country to find a viable solution to the problem. One of the leading industrial fortnightlies, i.e. *Industrial Times,* Mumbai (now extinct) conducted a symposium in 1978 and sought views from some of the private sector elite CEOs against the following questionnaire :

i) What is your reaction to the proposal of the Janta government to put a ceiling on the remuneration of management? How far would such measures contribute to a an alternative to narrow the disparities in employee remuneration in the corporate sector in general?

II) Is it reasonable to bring about parity in the emoluments of executives in the public and private sectors, considering the different systems of operation of the two sectors?

III) Could you outline the prerequisites for a uniform system of managerial remuneration for similar responsibilities, involving the same level of competence and capability? How do you rate the feasibility of such an exercise?

iv) What repercussions would such curbs have on management culture and industrial relations practices? Would they contribute to higher productivity? What would their ramifications be on the pattern of investment, production and demand, and on the economy in general?

While one of the chief executives stated that parity is inequitable in regard to the payment of wages to the CEOs in private and public sector enterprises, yet another MD remarked that any limitation on the quantum of emoluments would prove to be a damper to motivation. The third CEO, who in addition to being the managing director of a major pharmaceutical company, was also considered to be a management 'guru', expressed the views that let market forces decide the package. He even mentioned that a ceiling on remuneration would be unjustified. Another chief stated that it would be advisable to standardize the emoluments. He even averred that the emoluments of a CEO constitute only a small percentage of the total operating expenses of an enterprise. The fifth CEO stated that putting a ceiling on a CEO's wage would amount to perpetuating occupational discrimination. The sixth one argued that incomes should be equated with the prices prevalent in different regions of the country. The author of this book also contributed a leading article on the subject.

Subsequently, under the Company's Act limits have been prescribed at different times in India. For instance, in the Schedule 13 of Companies Act a CEO of a public owned company with an effective capital of Rs. one crore is to be paid Rs 75000 per month. In the case of Rs. 100 crore the comapny emoluments have been fixed at Rs. 2 lakhs per month. Besides, performance of a company has been taken as the basis in other cases. For a private company a CEO's package comprising fixed pay, variables and commission should not exceed 5 per cent of the profits. Within these provisions and a limit of 11 per cent of profits on total emoluments of all the directors the late Mr. Dhirubhai Ambani and his two sons Anil and Mukesh between themselves enjoyed a pacakage of Rs. 23 crore per year.

While the author has analysed the practice of formulation of package in the public sector undertakings in the previous chapter, some other people have recently suggested that a CEO's package should not exceed 15 times the wages of a worker in the company. As against this, in the US a CEO's package varies from 400 to 500 times of a worker in some firms. This aspect has caused great anxiety among the shareholders and the public at large. Even in European countries, a CEO's emoluments could vary from 50 to 100 times of the lowest paid worker in different enterprises. In Russia, during the communist regime, the highest paid CEO would draw 4 to 5 times of the lowest paid worker.

Hence the point at issue is as to what factors should be taken into reckoning for deciding the emoluments of a CEO. Perhaps, the following points may hold some relevance on this vexed issue:

i) The factor of education, professional expertise, competence and experience as also the ability to set and achieve goals could be found valid in this regard.

ii) Linking of the reward system with the efforts invested and the results achieved.

iii) Adequage returns (percentage of profits above the bank interest) to the shareholders and ensuring sustainable growth of the enterprise.

iv) Maintaing some parity with the emoluments paid to the CEOs of MNCs operating within the country. This could be done by determining the purchasing power parity in dollar terms of the expatriate in his home country, say the US vis-a-vis the PPP of the rupee in India and other currencies in their respective home countries. A composite

PPP matrix could be developed for countries like the US, EU, Japan and India.

vi) The CEO should not be expected to operate as a 'sadhu' in CEO's garb as the material aspect cannot be ignored for a business executive, especially when even ordinary shopkeepers or wholesalers make millions without paying taxes and inviting public wrath. Material comforts virtually have a vice-like grip on humans as even popular sadhus and priests fall prey to the temptation of AC/Air travel, Five-Star hotel stay, red carpet reception, glory and material possessions. The less said the better about a politician's illegal income.

In any case, the process of determining the wages of a CEO has to be an ongoing exercise in the context of social, economic and political developments as also the pattern of wages obtaining in different parts of the world. Yet, there is a need to avoid creation of islands of prosperity within a sea of poverty.

CHAPTER - 32

Role Stress Leads to Executive Burnout

The phenomenon of executive burnout was noticed a few decades ago by some management experts, especially the ones with a background in psychology and psychiatry. Some of the symptoms manifest in a large segment of executives related to exhaustion, withdrawal, job alienation, plateaued performance, unsocial behaviour, indifferent to state of affairs in the organization, lowering of morale, demotivation, peculiar body language and cynical attitude. In many cases, a sort of abnormalcy was also observed in work-life balance. So much so, that some of the executives specially at higher levels were charged with neglect of their families as well as their own lives. Some of the dominant physical disorders like indigestion, frequent headache, insomnia, loss of appetite, rising blood pressure, depression and so on were also observed. In many a cases, a feeling of worthlessness too was noticed amongst executives. Earlier in some cases this phenomenon was considered to be an extension of mid-life crises, owing to frustration to achieve career-related goals at the middle or senior levels. But later, the symptoms of burnout were even observed amongst the CEOs. Perhaps, some of them could not stand the heat at the apex.

Obviously, in a situation like this, the performance level of the organization declined drastically. Their loss of interest in work led to a negative state of mind. As a result of loss of psychological anchor and snapping of ties with the active world of work and organization, their minds got completely distracted from the objective and purpose of their very presence in the organization. Their self-image suffered a setback not only in their own mind but even in the eyes of peers, bosses, subordinates and other related people.

Considering the above situation and pervasive effect of

this phenomena, corporates started taking recourse to a number of interventions either in the shape of inside mentoring or counselling arranged through outside consultants. Some of the factors and processes which were emphasized to rectify the situation related to education of executives in the area of self-analysis, confidence-building, revival of interest in job and life and various other related issues. The main focus of such interventions was on corrective measures designed to change the behaviour pattern and attitude of the individuals.

A few interventions put more emphasis on the process of morale boosting, motivation, better management of time scheduling of activities, promotion of team work, better communication and interpersonal relationship. Special attention was also paid to the vital aspect of work-life balance.

While corporate efforts were being concentrated on the various corrective measures, change in the business intensity of competition, restructuring of the corporation and business units, higher level of customer aspiration, change in the role expectations of CEOs, major changes in the business policies by the government and the rising size and expectations of the various stakeholders brought about a radical shift in the business-related strategies and operating practices. This put a tremendous strain on the minds of the top executives and the resources of the organization. Virtually, a paradigm shift in the total corporate scenario made itself manifest. In fact, one after another brutal shifts in the mode of doing business within the country and abroad, created a burden on the chief executives in terms of pressure of time, excessive travelling, networking and lack of rest and leisure resulted in further worsening of the situation. Keeping away from the family and friends and the social circle deprived the top executives from socializing and entertainment.

Hardly had the corporates evolved measures and designed strategies to cope with the complex and strenuous situation, yet another onslaught in the shape of scams, scandals and consequent loss of trust and confidence of the community and the stakeholders in the chief executives, the board of directors and other senior executives resulted in loss of face and image of the corporation and consequent burnout of the badly scarred chief executives.

As already observed in the case of the US, most of the CEOs have become scared of the prevailing situation and trying their utmost to wriggle out of the situation either by lying low or by seeking support of the community with a view to lead a calm, quiet and peaceful life. One thing which needs to be watched is the cascading effect on the morale of the executives lower down in the hierarchy of the corporation. If such conditions persist for a long time, the number of cases of executive burnout particularly at the level of CEOs are likely to multiply.

It is, therefore, necessary that the various agencies like government, the politicians, the community and the stakeholders join hands to control the rot. May be the corporate CEOs should take a cue from the pious disposition of their counterparts in the non-profit NGOs and observe the code of conduct usually prescribed and followed by the latter as true trustees of the society. Roles have to be distinct and job-specific, yet a positive mental attitude removed from the excessive lure of the lucre will help them to avoid burnout and meet the challenge and pressures of the job fairly and squarely.

Management gurus, academicians, practising CEOs acting as guest speakers and the various corporate federations, chambers and associations will have to change their tone and tenor regarding strategies and measures aimed at out manoeuvring business rivals and eulogizing the motto of survival of the fittest. Perhaps, a collaborative approach in corporate life might help the situation.

CHAPTER – 33

How to Avoid Executive Burnout

In the previous chapter the various symptoms associated with the phenomenon of executive burnout were spelt out. Some of the consequences, especially the ones resulting in plateaued performance of an individual were also highlighted. Whether it is the changing complex of the business scenario or the various socio-economic-cum-political factors which catapult a business organization into a highly vulnerable situation or enactment of rules and regulations to enforce order and control the deviant behaviour of the various enterprises in the country, are the factors which could cause additional burden on the working life of executives in an organization. Even in the event of a slow process of change which is mainly evolutionery in nature, scope and depth, the element of strain and stress on the executives cannot be ruled out, as various other associated factors at individual and enterprise level continue to plague the mind of the executives. Whether it is India, Japan, USA or any other country the executives are constantly exposed to the influence of these viatal forces.

At the individual level, the various factors which have a deep impact on the physical and mental state of an individual could be enumerated as under :

Fear of Failure: By virtue of mental set up certain individuals, particularly executives at top level harbour a constant fear of failure. It needs to be emphasized that success and failure are two aspects of working life and when a myopic view is taken of either of these an anomalous situation emerges. It may be pointed out that while effectiveness is a function of a string of successes, yet an element of failure cannot be ruled out on certain occasions. Whether it is the celebrities, transformation leaders or high achievers they too have to confront failure/s at one stage or the other in their lives. People with firm resolve, consider failures as pillars of success and continue to combat them with latent potential, grit and dedication. Once this reality takes root, the fear of failure no longer dogs the mind and causes frustration.

Work-Life Balance: Usually when an executive sets his foot on the corporate soil, he harbours a robust ambition to scale the hierarchy in double quick time. While it may be all right for a bachelor young executive to pay more attention to his job with some amount of time earmarked for regular exercise, yet for a married executive it is essential to devote time to his family which could provide peace, tranquillity, satisfaction and a stress-free work life. In fact, the nagging feeling of guilt for ignoring the family vanishes from the mind and removes tension to a great extent. Those required to travel frequently need to watch food intake and avoid over indulgence. At 71, when I look back at my corporate career in a multinational, public sector and private sector, spanning almost 4-1/2 decades and maintaining a balance between life and work, especially by virtue of regular exercise and an absorbing hobby, even while carrying tremendous job load in the public sector, gives me a tremendous satisfaction. I am sure any individual, especially a CEO can do that with profit by observing this simple regime in life.

Realistic Outlook: One must have a reality check of the situation at different stages of life by comparing his personality profile with the job requirements and strike a balance between what possibly he could achieve under the circumstances. This will eradicate all the illusions from the mind and help avoiding mismatch between him and the job. This will also eliminate negative emotions and minimize rivalry and peer jealousy from the mind and avoid frustration and burnout.

The organization could create a congenial and comfortable working environment for the executives in some of the following ways :

Selection and Placement : Keeping in view the requirements of a job, the organization should strive to hire suitable candidates rather than the ones who are over qualified. This process needs to be reviewed at different stages of working life of an executve in the organization. Moreover, instead of providing a deceptive career trajectory a range of career paths unrelated with the rat race could be chartered.

Man-Job-Match: The man-job-match is a very vital feature of smooth sailing in an organization. This means the individual profile has to be matched with the job profile of the organization. While the individual profile could be sketched in terms of education, training, experience, expertise emotional quotient aptitude for a particular type of activity, the job profile portrays requirements in terms of the nature of the job, tasks and elements as also the nature of technology, work processes and organizational culture. As such, it is essential that these two aspects are matched to the extent possible to avoid dissonance between these two entities. It has been observed that mismatched individuals get disenchanted sooner or later and start exhibiting signs of deep frustration and burnout.

Executive Development : Short duration breaks from the routine job help considerably the executives to socialize, interact, relax and network with colleagues from different parts of the plateaued country, especially when the organization operates over a vast territory. This would ensure improved continuous learning, unlearning development and save the executives from getting plateaued. Denied promotion to a deserving executive also plays havoc. Of course, deadwood has to be weeded out.

Appraisal System : It is a fact of life, that the organization-related processes keep on evolving. Accordingly, the appraisal system too has travelled a long way from confidential reporting to the 360 appraisal system. This system has yet to prove its efficacy and reliability as it is likely to put a great strain on the mind of an individual and shift his focus from task orientation to relationship and disturb the delicate balance. Those unable to cope with this process are likely to feel inadequate and insecure. CEOs being exposed widely to large organizational segments are likely to be more vulnerable.

Stretch Targets : Some time back the Club of Rome came out with the thesis of limits to growth. This concept has a considerable element of truth as setting up of higher targets year after year in terms of production, sales and growth is putting a great strain not only on the natural resources of a country but even on the minds of the executives as those unable to cope with the over stretched targets, due to intense competition from other organizations and availability of substitutes and fakes, could set a serious limit on the market demand. It is, therefore, essential that the organizations do not insist on irrationally high targets.

To cap it all, the corporates and especially the CEOs must operate on the basis of ground reality rather than the stock market graphs and curves. This will remove illusion from their minds and reduce the chances of associated mental and physical strain and consequent burnout. There is also a dire need to maintain equilibrium between a materialistic and spiritualistic outlook.

Part III

Case Histories

CASE HISTORY-1

Ethics in Business

Though the process of industrialization started some three centuries ago, yet the present century has witnessed the widest ever exposure of business to the environment in the shape of political conditions, the economic situation, social norms, value systems, religious codes and many other factors.

These factors impose a great strain on the minds of business entrepreneurs in the industrialized world as also economically backward regions. The position becomes all the more complex when the businessman brought up in a particular environment has to confront the value systems projected by the society vis-à-vis his own values, beliefs and codes. This way he has to assume a countenance of innocence and high morals even by contradicting his own professed standards in an effort to strike a compromise with the social situation.

As it is, the ethical standards of a man are influenced by a number of factors like ego, education, sex, position in the society, political climate, the level of economic activity and advancement, the cultural orientation of the society, the interaction of the people with outsiders, i.e. the nationals of other countries and so on. In fact, in the earlier stages of life ethics are moulded by the influence of the mother, father, teacher, the classmates, the playmates and so on. The place of entry in business or job as also the time of entry too govern the ethical behaviour, where the code of conduct to a great extent imposes on the individual high norms of behaviour like dedication, sincerity, commitment and trust in the people and the organization. The behaviour of an individual takes a positive direction in its approach and relationship with others.

On the other hand, in a corrupt, demoralized and

unorganized society the behaviour of the individual gets conditioned by certain objective courses which might contradict the needs of business, the society, the government and the country at large. Obviously, the response to the need of the customer in terms of quality of product, standard of service and safety are seriously jeopardized. In fact, the system becomes unresponsive to each other's demands as both the business community and their clients operate at cross purposes. In a situation like this, the businessman gets lost and does not know how to operate.

Real Life Situation

A peculiar situation like this arises often when, a particular individual brought up in a specific environment of high morals, faces an entirely different situation. This could happen either, when a business entrepreneur enters service or when the entrepreneur or an executive opts out of business. It may be worthwhile to narrate a real life story to bring home the point of ethics, which, at times could result in giving rude shocks to the morality of an individual. The following story though portrays a real life situation, yet the names indicated are fictitious.

Mr. Harris hailed from a middle class family, his father being a junior level official in a State Government Department. The family environment of Mr. Harris emphasized high moral standards, ethical behaviour and total dedication and sincerity to work. It also valued a direct approach and high level of trust with each other in the family environment. The members valued earnestness, honesty and good behaviour in day-to-day interaction with each other. Disciplined disposition and respectful attitude towards equals and elders were treated as heavenly virtues. Mr. Harris received his Master's degree in Geophysics from one of the renowned technical institutes of the country.

In the early 1960s by the time he completed his education, he lost interest in his area of training and professional preparation. He therefore opted for the Police service and subsequently for the post of Management Trainee in a business firm. The main objective of rejecting the Police job was to keep out of the bureaucratic life and to be free from corruption, malpractice and underhand means of livelihood. Another reason for avoiding the Police job, as often professed by him was, that the Police service breeds cruelty, indifference and callousness. It also disregards human dignity and good social behaviour.

After having gained his Management training, Mr. Harris finally grabbed the job of a Purchase Officer in one of the Public Sector organizations. He continued in the job for about 7 years and thereafter opted out for the post of a Manager Purchase in a private company, dealing with the manufacture marketing and sales of trucks and other automobiles. By dint of his hard work, sincerity, devotion and good relationship with the peers, bosses and suppliers, he earned six spurs in a short span of seven years and rose to the rank of General Manager (Material). Being straight forward, tough and aggressive, at times, he would rub shoulders with executives of other disciplines of the organization. Over time, he happened to strain his relationship with the senior bosses whose ethical standards, values and chemistry somehow did not match his own. Being unable to continue in the strained and tension-torn situation, he decided to give up the job and opted out of the business. While in service, he had earned the reputation of being honest and objective and the entire market regarded him as an astute buyer in the corporate world. Surprisingly, the Chairman of his corporation had given him a letter of recognition and a big cash award just before he left the job. This, not only surprised his colleagues but also the suppliers and other people around him.

Moral Dilemma

His real dilemma began when, he went out in the open, struggling for entry in a suitable business line. One of the leading firms, dealing with various products like textiles, synthetics, fertilizers and machineries not only offered him a big job but also kept him on a retainer basis for periodical consultancy in the area of materials management. This arrangement enabled him to earn sufficient income to support his family while pursuing his business activity.

As he had made some contracts, with some of the business men in the private sector, one of his friends came forward to enter into a partnership for starting the business of video cassette taping. As the technology was not available within the country, both the equipment and the know-how had to be imported from Japan and Korea. Mr. Harris' partner accompanied him to Japan and Korea for the purchase of the equipment as also to learn the technology and the know-how of video cassette taping.

As ill luck would have it, the partnership broke up within a span of six months after an initial investment of Rs. 7 lakhs in foreign trips and initial purchases. During this period, Mr. Harris experienced many cultural shocks on account of the major transformation in his style of life, relationship with the people, dealings with the government officials and others. In fact, while he had not taken a single penny in the shape of bribes during his service career, he was compelled to bribe people at every step for the movement of files and papers in the government offices. The initial licence alone for entering into the video cassette taping business cost him a few lakhs of rupees. Subsequently, at every step say the Customs Office, the Import & Export Office, the rail transport office, the Airlines for that matter every single office or institution he came across, he had to invest a substantial amount of speed money.

At times, he would get qualms of conscience and turn to his friends for guidance and consolation. Often, his friends would counsel him for not taking rigid stances on such earthly issues and take a practical view of life. The saying goes, "Do in Rome as the Romans do. According to them, this would be the normal code of conduct which must necessarily be observed by the men willing to make some headway in business.

Philosopher's Version

They would often quote John Kenneth Galbraith, the noted economist and statesman according to whom business enterprises are to pursue objectives that are rational and purely economic; and it is the regulatory nature of law and the political process–rather than the invisible hand of the market place–that would turn these objectives to the common good. Galbraith also averred that the moral direction for business decision-making is supposed to be provided by political managers who are the custodians of the Public Purpose.

They would also quote Goodpastor and Matthews, according to whom it is "the system" that is expected to provide moral direction; and as such the business has no moral responsibility beyond political and legal obedience. This way both the views, that of Galbraith and Goodpastor and Matthews locate morality, ethics, responsibility and conscience in the system of rules and incentives in which the modern business finds itself embedded. Both the views thus reject the exercise of independent moral judgement by business corporations in the society. However, one glaring difference between the two standpoints is, that, one recognizes the invisible moral forces of the market and, the other looks to the visible moral forces in the government. This way, these philosophers externalize the moral restraint and exonerate the business comunity from responsibility to impose internal constraints on their behaviour. Rather, they refuse to recognize the business community as a moral agent in the society. A deeper insight, however, repels this thesis, neither the "invisible hand" of the market nor "visible hand" of the government regulations can be finally relied upon to provide an adequate safeguard against moral laxity of business. In fact, these external forces of restraint can at best constitute a useful second line of defence. The inability of market forces to resolve such moral issues is also well-known. What is not sufficiently appreciated is that governmental regulatory agencies too have intrinsic limitations. In a democratic free market society, it is difficult to believe that the regulatory agency could have adequate knowledge and the resources to cope with the various developments in the areas of technology and processes in the industry, which would be easily screened and certified as safe from the point of society. Moreover, the magnitude of such progress is baffling as the developments in the product processes and inventions keep taking place simultaneously in different parts of the world and in different industries. The problem gets complicated further, as the governments are often deeply involved and implicated in the technology and business corporations they are expected to control. Under the circumstances, it is difficult to ensure that the business community will act with the highest standard of responsibility and care when the technologies and processes these corporations control can have devastating consequences for the people.

Moreover, when corporate managers take decisions that might endanger other people's lives, how can we be sure that, the risk they expose others to are going to be acceptable risks ? Hence, when the entrepreneurs weigh the risks and benefits of their decisions, what is the guarantee that what seems "rational" to the business will also be "right" for the community.

Friendly Advice

Advice doled out by his old friends as also his college teachers and professors were not much different from the ones given by his present day friends.

After the first phase was over, and the partnership broke up with his business associate, Mr. Harris started a frantic search for having some people either from the friendly circle or outside to enter into a partnership with him. The partner had to play the role of a financier while Mr. Harris was to keep to himself the role of a working partner as well as Executive Director of the firm. Initially, Mr. Harris put up his Taping Plant in one of the suburban areas near the capital city of a state. As production and sales progressed he decided to put up another unit in the neighbouring state. While the first unit was to produce plain tapes, in the second unit he decided to pack the recorded tapes in the cassettes. This decision was based on the general market preference for the recorded tapes, especially the ones recorded with movie films. For producing this type of tapes machines had to be imported again from Japan. As the various hurdles like obtaining an import licence, foreign exchange clearance, technical clearance and customs clearance had to be crossed in successive measures, the old process of pumping in speed money at every stop had to be repeated with considerable strain on his conscience.

With the operation of the units, the business prospects virtually boomed and he was able to grab massive orders for a large number of cassettes from the open market in the surrounding areas. He had hardly finished the first lot of the orders, when a sudden shift took place in the government policy in regard too videos on account of lobbying by the film industry against 'video piracy'.

In fact, an act was passed in the Parliament, by virtue of which, the video piracy was declared a cognizable offence and the people indulging in the production and marketing of video tapes would render themselves liable for fine and confinement.

With this onslaught, the production units came to a grinding halt and the market collapsed. Not only did the machines, the raw materials and the semi-finished products pile up but even the inventory of the finished tapes remained unsold. Mr. Harris thus became upset and was unable to reckon as to what course of action he should take to save his family, his employees and his units from utter ruin. Under these compulsions, he had to borrow money from the banks at high rates and thus underwent heavy debts.

Friends and business allies came forward with flashy ideas and suggestions for price cuts, dilution in quality, under invoicing production, dodging the excise and sales authorities and all such measures reflecting business practices of the market.

His friends would often quote the well-known philosopher John Ladd who puts it this way, "we cannot and must not accept formal organizations, or their representatives acting in their official capacity, to be honest, courageous, considerate, sympathetic, or to have any kind of moral integrity. Such concepts are not in the vocabulary, so to speak of the organization language game." But, when Harris was reminded of Peter Drucker the implications of the view points expressed by John Ladd would have disastrous implications. According to Drucker, "in a society of organization" such as ours in which both individual and social well-being is affected to such a large extent by the conduct of powerful business corporations "sincerity" or otherwise of these organizations, is perhaps one of the central problems of our time. yet at the same time Drucker was at pains to say that in contemporary discussions the problem was not even seen.

But Mr. Harris was soon reminded by his friend Milton Friedman, according to whom the true and only social responsibility of business organization is to make profit and obey the laws. The workers of the free and competitive market place will 'moralize' corporate behaviour quite independently of any direct attempts to moralize and transform corporate decision-making. A deliberate morality in the making of business decisions is encouraged in the name of systematic morality, the common good is best served whom each of us in our economic institution pursued not the common good or moral purpose, but competitive advantage. As such in this view, morality, responsibility and conscience reside in the "invisible hand" of the free market system and not in the hands of business organizations within the system, much less the entrepreneurs or managers within the organization. Any advice that moral adjustment be accorded with corporate strategy, is seen as insufficient and arrogant and in the end both an illegitimate use of corporate power and abuse of entrepreneurs/managers fiduciary role.

No doubt Mr. Harris went into an "ethical coma" and his mind got baffled further.

Shattered Mind

These developments shattered Mr. Harris' faith in his perceptions about business ethics professed even by the reputed organizations who had a long history of high moral codes about their business dealings with the shareholders, employees, government and the consumers. Some of them had even built features into their management incentive system, board structures, internal control systems and research agencies that in a person we would call self- control, integrity and conscientiousness. He would also think of others who had institutionalized awareness and concern for consumers, employees and the various publics.

He got convinced to a great extent that almost every business man possessed double standards, in terms of a written and professed code and the actual business practices. This also confirmed his conception that even though the elder business men displayed a high level of ethical awareness of business yet, they somehow felt compelled to take recourse to some of the anti-social practices. The recent happenings soon flashed back on his mind where, various malpractices were uncovered in the textile industry and vegetable oils which indulged in anti-social activities like adulteration and other nefarious practices.

In spite of visible manifestations of corruption and malpractices in the business world his mind refused to accept this as an all pervasive situation in the business world. His mind would tell, that, some of the industries like construction, engineering and certain businesses like banking, investment and insurance, no doubt had a tarnished image about their business ethics, yet there were many other areas of business activity like manufacturing and trading where the image of industry still remained untarnished.

The second partner, who had joined him a few months ago, became disillusioned with the partnership and started pressurizing Mr. Harris for the repayment of his debt. Mr. Harris made frantic contact with his relations and friends, placed in high positions in government and industry here and there, and, sought their advice for picking up a few items for production or for outright trading. A few offers also came his way, for taking a job in the area of materials management, in which he had considerable experience and expertise before switching over to business.

Switch Over

On the advice of one of his highly placed friends in the coal industry, Mr. Harris decided to book orders for the sale of coal and coke in the northern region of the country which happened to be located quite far from the producing areas. Being unfamiliar with the tricks of the trade of coal, he suffered some shocks initially both in terms of finance and ethics. This happened, as, the various agents and traders involved in the coal business had the record of not being clean in their dealings and disposition. Even though Mr. Harris' mental barrier had been demolished to a great extent, against unethical practices of the business worked, yet, he would console himself from the facts that ultimately when he was able to establish himself in the line he would prepare a code of conduct for his own firm and employees and would follow the traditions of some reputable companies of the country, who, believed in straight dealings and honest practices.

He believed that there can be no such guarantee, nor any single easy route to corporate responsibility. What one can do is to create a context for corporate decision-making within which the 'right' decision becomes more likely. The only approach that goes to the root of the matter is one that seeks to introduce a powerful restraining and deterring factor capable of influencing corporate managers in the very act of taking risk-prone decisions, namely, the prospect of having to personally face the consequences of negligence in taking such decisions results in serious harm to others. The development of certain new doctrines and applications in criminal law perhaps offer the most promising means of introducing corporate managers to behave responsibly and to decide rightly. But what is a 'right' decision? How does one recognize a responsible decision from an irresponsible or reckless one?

He was again reminded of Goodpastor and Matthews who show that it is quite possible to define the underlying processes that constitute 'responsible' behaviour and that those processes are the same for individuals as for organizations. They identify two traits which characterize responsible behaviour; respect and rationality. Taking a morally responsible point of view includes respecting persons as ends and not as means or as things, that is, going beyond seeing others merely as instrumental to accomplishing one's own purposes. It implies a conscious concern for the effects of one's decisions and actions on others, and taking their needs and interests seriously. Secondly, moral responsibility also includes features we usually attribute top rational decision-making, that is, foresight, lack of impulsiveness, care in mapping out alternatives and their consequences, fundamental clarity about goals and purposes, and careful attention to details of implementation.

In the coal trade, the price structure is highly flexible and the rates for different grades of coal keep varying from day to day. Besides, the different varieties of coal like hard coke, pearl coke, etc. command a very high premium in the market.

In a bid to capture the market and project an image of honest businessman, he entered into price deals with some of the buyers of coal. Soon after the stock was dispatched from the production centres, he came to realize that his cost price was higher than the selling price, he was committed to. This not only reflected his inexperienced disposition in the coal business, but also indicated his lack of business acumen to comprehend the total situation in the coal trade. However, he soon recovered from this situation and made a quick survey of the price structure and started making some marginal gains in the coal trade.

Initially, he decided to entertain orders only on the basis

of cash payment but the reality of the situation did not warrant this approach and, he was compelled to entertain the various buyers on credit terms. True to the spirit of unethical business practices, some of the buyers did not care to pay the price for the stock so bought from Mr. Harris. This was yet another typical practice in the coal trade, which he did not realize or, apprehend in the initial stage.

In course of time, Mr. Harris got used to the situation and made the requisite adjustments to adopt some of the practices being followed in the coal trade. This at least assured his survival in the business world, though at a high price of moral and ethical compromise.

CASE HISTORY-2

Longing for Corporated Decision-Making

Ram Nath obtained a degree in business management from IIM Bangalore in 1995. On the basis of a campus interview, he got job offer from a multinational at a salary of Rs. 50 lakhs per annum. At the same time he was also considering other offers which could have landed easily in his lap from the Indian corporate sector. The going wage rate on an average was Rs. 7 lakh per annum as against Rs. 20 lakh offered to exceptionally good students by one of the leading organizations in India. The other option available to Ram Nath was joining his father's (Gian Chand) business at Agra.

The company was dealing in leather and leather products with a turnover of Rs. 70 crore per annum. While his father was keen that Ram Nath should join family business the latter was not so anxious to get into the leather business. This was so, as two younger brothers of Ram Nath had almost completed degree level education and would be available for sharing their father's responsibility. Ram Nath was rather keen that his brothers who did not have much prospects of a lucrative career in the corporate world could avail themselves of the opportunity of joining the family business and thereby make a substantial contribution to its growth. He also surmised that he could always render help and guidance to his brothers as also assist his father in running the affairs of business. Since he had specialized in international marketing, he could even render advice to his family in the export of leather products, which had attained good quality standards by this time.

In spite of the fact that the business was running satisfactorily, yet he was not very happy about the process of decision-making at the level of top management as well as other ranks down below. In fact, the process of decision-making confined mainly to the family circles and most of the vital decisions were taken by the promoter himself. Not only Ram Nath but even Gian Chand, his father, were fully conscious of the fact that some drastic changes were required in the area of decision-making. Even though Gian Chand was not aware of the theories, models, support system and various other modern concepts regarding decision-making, yet based on his hunch, instincts and readily available facts and figures, he was able to take decisions. However, the growth of business and its expansion to the foreign markets necessitated a formal professional approach to the process of decision-making.

This was one area, which, Gian Chand realized where, his eldest son Ram Nath could help in a big way. He could at least educate his brothers and the various professionals in the functional areas like production, finance, marketing, as well as logistics with regard to the nature, type and scope of decisions involved in these areas. He could also help them to analyse the modus operandi of the various functions, the organization structure, reporting relationship and the alignment of decision-making process in this regard. At least, he could have educated them about the particular categories of decisions and the type of decisions like operational, supervisory and strategic relevant for the various levels in functional hierarchy. He could also expose them to the concept of the impact of decisions in the enterprise. Obviously, decisions having the largest and pervasive impact need to be taken by the CEO and others having functional impact for a particular division or department could be taken by the respective heads.

He could also make them aware of the fact that when the organization grows and attains diversity in terms of products and markets, the load of decisions and the need for taking urgent decisions requires proper distribution of decision load through the process of delegation of powers. In other words, adequate delegation would be a necessary pre-condition for successful operation of business.

While Ram Nath took up an assignment with an MNC with an initial posting in Paris, he continued to guide his brothers and other professionals of the company in this regard. In fact, he even got initiated a formal training programme in the area of decision-making for different levels in the corporate hierarchy. He also advised his father to render active support to the process of training and education of the executives of the company. No doubt, within a span of a year a significant improvement was noticed in the area of decision-making of the enterprise.

In the meantime, after having been with the MNC for almost half a decade, Ram realized that in a large corporation one gets stuck in the rigmarole of day-to-day routine and mostly have to carry out the commands of the bosses. Most of the decisions relating to strategy and managerial activity are confined to the senior managerial levels and one does not get much autonomy and freedom to give full expression to one's faculties and well rounded development of corporate personality. Besides, he also missed the excitement and emotional involvement in a system where it was difficult to have a corporate level look and exposure to the big picture, which one aspires to in the corporate life.

Thus, influenced by the notion of autonomy and the desire to be a part of the system which could compensate him for all he had missed in a paid job, he decided to repatriate to his country and join the family business.

Obviously, with his exposure to the exotic culture and the way of doing business in an MNC, he could convince his father about his ability to manage the export of leather goods to the European countries effectively. On joining the family business as one of the directors he had all the opportunities to associate himself with the vital business activity and the process of taking strategic decisions at his level which could help to shape the destiny of the family enterprise.

CASE HISTORY-3

The Problem of Corporate Succession

Raman was working in government as an engineer. He had picked up the job soon after acquiring an engineering degree from a reputed institution in northern India. After having been in the job for a few years, he realized that his destiny lay somewhere else. In fact, even his colleagues had observed that Raman would have been more successful in business. Therefore, considering the fact that the government job offered limited opportunities for advancement and meagre pay, he would often talk to his father about the need for a change. His father usually asked him one question about whether he had made up his mind for a change to business. He would also ask him of his choice for any particular occupation, which would suit his temperament and bear ample fruits of his labour and investment.

Today after 25 years, when Raman's mind goes down memory lane he feels that he had made the right decision with regard to quitting the job and opting out for an independent occupation. This is so, as growth of his business has been rather steady and continuous. Even though there have been rough patches owing to change in the market situation for the various products he had been manufacturing in his factories, yet on the whole progress has been satisfactory. During the span of these two and a half decades, the growth curve witnessed two distinct phases. While during the first ten years his company could attain a turnover of nearly Rs. 80 to 90 crores, yet the next ten years were marked by rapid strides in growth. During this period the turn over touched a reasonable level and could be considered almost at par with some of the leading enterprises in the northern region excepting a few corporate giants and MNCs which were operating with much higher turnover. Yet, a turnover of Rs. 1000 crore could be considered fairly good for taking the enterprise to still higher reaches provided the enthusiastic spirit of the entrepreneur continued to guide him in his strategy, plans and operating practices.

By the time the company had reached this level, it had built up a viable functional structure with all the divisions and departments suitably manned by qualified engineers, executives and other professionals. The various corporate policies and procedures too had been evolved and embodied in the manuals. These manuals helped the various professionals as also the fresh hands in understanding their checks and controls, delegation of powers and their accountability.

The organization's manual incorporated details about functional distribution, job profiles and lines of growth of the executives from the point of intake to the successively higher positions in the corporate hierarchy. However, the apex envisaged for each function usually terminated at the level of a GM or an executive director. In some functions the position of a director also obtained especially for rewarding loyalty and long tenure in the company. Despite this, one thing was clear to everyone that in a family-sowned business especially in India, the reins of top management would always remain in the hands of members of the family.

Raman was quite aware of these facts and the prevailing practices in the country. He was also conscious of the fact that the large empire he had built up by virtue of his vision, imagination, hard labour and capital could not be handed over to the outside professionals who did not have an emotional stake in the enterprise due to limited interest. Virtually, their stake was confined to the prospects of continuity of the job and payment of regular emoluments. Therefore, when he entered middle age, he started contemplating the subject of succession for his enterprise.

Even though he had two children who had been well-groomed by virtue of education and training to take up responsible positions in the company, yet he was doubtful about their continued interest in the type of business he had developed. In fact, the products manufactured in some of the factories represented the brick and mortar type of business which is usually shunned by the modern generation. While he was worried that his son would not continue with the enterprise despite all the attention and efforts focused on his learning and development in the case of his daughter, the country's tradition of not sharing business assets and responsibilities with the female members stood in the way. Obviously, in India the women become part of another family after marriage.

Raman thus faced a serious problem in terms of his succession. In the meantime, due to a slump in the industry and a drastic reduction in demand for various products he was confronted with a grave situation. Some of the units started losing heavily. Thus his son who was handling these production units got disillusioned with the business. In the process, some of the senior executives including general managers became demoralized with the state of affairs. Quite a few put in their papers and parted company with the enterprise. This also led to trouble with the trade unions and the workers. Some of them left on their own with meagre compensation, while others felt compelled to leave the company, as there was no work and wages.

On rough reckoning, Raman realized that his assets and liabilities were almost in balance and he could continue to manage the business single-handedly even if his son left the organization. Soon after, his son started a new enterprise in the IT area and the daughter went abroad a few years after her marriage. He also reckoned that the plant and equipment in the various factories, which had been closed, could give him some returns. Besides, the land and other infrastructure developed around the factories would also bring enough money on disposal. Moreover, he had accumulated considerable wealth and immovable property in the shape of agriculture land and residential accommodation in posh localities of the metropolis to take care of not only his lifetime requirements but even of those from the next one or two generations.

Incidentally, Raman continued to manage one or two factories, which were still profitable and perhaps would get closed after he was unable to manage the business physically owing to the age factor. Anyone who has been familiar with his business philosophy could make out that he would prefer to sell business rather than to hand it over to non-family professionals. Under the circumstances, an enterprise which had once grown to a massive size with fair prospects of future growth would vanish soon from the industrial horizon due to lack of succession. Perhaps, Raman could make yet another attempt to persuade his son to save the situation.

Index